Lists

The
Book

BK1001

Other Books By Derric Johnson

I DIDN'T KNOW THAT
People, Places, Customs and Things
That Bind Americans Together

EASY DOESN'T DO IT
A Challenging Call for
Commitment to Excellence.

TABLE OF CONTENTS

SECTION THREE
HUMOR

SECTION FOUR
LEADERSHIP

SECTION FIVE
MUSIC

SECTION SIX
PATRIOTIC

SECTION SEVEN
POLITICS

SECTION EIGHT
RANDOM INFORMATION

SECTION NINE
RELATIONSHIPS

SECTION TEN
RELIGION

SECTION ELEVEN
SEASONAL

SECTION TWELVE
SENIORS

SECTION THIRTEEN
SERVICE

SECTION FOURTEEN
SUCCESS

SECTION FIFTEEN
WORDS

SECTION SIXTEEN
THE WORK PLACE

INTRODUCTION

Technically, a list is setting forth in order any series of names or items. A list is a series of any kind, no matter what the arrangement or purpose. It can be an index, catalogue, inventory, roster or register.

But to a public speaker, a list can be used in any presentation as... a humorous introduction

a thought-provoking illustration
a transitional moment
a significant statement
an inspiring concept
or a stirring conclusion.

Lists have become some of my best friends in communication. This book contains one hundred and thirty (that's lots of lists for laughs and lifts) that have helped me through thousands of speeches

talks
devotionals
sermons
lectures
lessons
recitations
orations
discourses
and addresses.

In this book you will find the lists basically categorized in 16 different sections, listed in the <u>TABLE OF CONTENTS</u> at the front of the collection.

Because so many of the lists have multiple uses, you will find an expanded <u>TOPICAL INDEX</u> in the back of the book.

Much of the material contained in this book was collected over a period of years from a variety of sources and has been used in a myriad of speaking engagements and in numerous printed articles. Many of the original authors are unknown and some of the lists have been attributed to more than one source. Since it is impossible to list each author, I would like this to stand as an acknowledgment of appreciation to the authors for the words of wit and wisdom contained in this book.

So now these lists are yours, to have and hold from this day forward. Use them carefully and often... they will serve you well.

DERRIC JOHNSON

Orlando, Florida

SECTION ONE

ONE

Commitment

WHATEVER HAPPENED TO ...

"Lovest thou me more than these?"

The early believers paid with their lives.

THE DISCIPLES

MATTHEW	martyred by the sword in Ethiopia
JOHN	escaped death in a cauldron of boiling oil then exiled on Patmos
JAMES, THE GREATER	beheaded in Jerusalem
JAMES, THE LESSER	thrown from the pinnacle of the Temple then beaten to death with clubs
BARTHOLOMEW	flayed alive
ANDREW	hanged on a cross where he preached till he died
THOMAS	run through the body with a lance in India
PETER	crucified upside down

THE OTHER FOLLOWERS

MARK	dragged through the streets of Alexandria
LUKE	hanged on an olive tree in Greece
MATHIAS	stoned, then beheaded
JUDE	shot to death with arrows
BARNABAS	stoned to death at Salonica
PAUL	beheaded at Rome by Emperor Nero

EVERYBODY... SOMEBODY...
ANYBODY... NOBODY...

This is a story about 4 people named
EVERYBODY,
SOMEBODY,
ANYBODY
and NOBODY.

There was an important job to be done and EVERYBODY was sure that SOMEBODY would do it. ANYBODY could have done it but NOBODY did it.

SOMEBODY got angry about that, because it was EVERYBODY'S job. EVERYBODY thought ANYBODY should do it, but NOBODY realized that EVERYBODY blamed SOMEBODY when NOBODY did what ANYBODY could have done.

These gentlemen were all neighbors but the way they lived was a shame. They all went to the same church but you never could have enjoyed worshipping with any of them.

EVERYBODY stayed home on Sundays to go fishing or to visit with his friends. ANYBODY wanted to worship but was afraid the SOMEBODY wouldn't speak to him. So . . . NOBODY went to church.

Actually, NOBODY was the only decent one of the four. NOBODY did all the church visitation and NOBODY volunteered anytime there was a church building or property work project.

And one day a Sunday School teacher was needed. EVERYBODY thought ANYBODY could do it. SOMEBODY thought EVERYBODY should. Guess who did . . . NOBODY!

And then one day a fifth neighbor moved in to live among them. EVERYBODY felt SOMEBODY should win him to Christ. ANYBODY could have at least made an effort. You want to guess who finally did win him? That's right . . . NOBODY!!

HEY! THERE'S HOPE FOR YOU

NEVER FINISHED GRADE SCHOOL

Mark Twain
Charles Dickens

NEVER FINISHED HIGH SCHOOL

Mary Baker Eddy
George Gershwin
Will Rogers
Both Wright Brothers
Peter Jennings

HAVE OR HAD LEARNING DISABILITIES

Tom Cruise
Bruce Jenner
O.J. Simpson
Cher
Hans Christian Anderson
Nelson Rockefeller
Woodrow Wilson
Leanardo da Vinci

Babe Ruth hit 714 home runs, but he also struck out 1,330 times.

A studio executive once dismissed **Fred Astaire** with the opinion: "Can't act... can't sing... balding... can dance a little."

Abraham Lincoln began the Blackhawk War as a captain, but by the end of the war he had been demoted to private.

Walt Disney was once fired by a newspaper editor because "he had no good ideas."

WHAT IS HUSTLE?

Hustle is doing something that everyone
   is absolutely certain can't be done

Hustle is getting the order because you get there first,
   or stayed with it after everyone else gave up

Hustle is shoe leather and elbow grease
                     and sweat
            and missing lunch

Hustle is getting prospects to say "yes"
   after they've said "no" twenty times

Hustle is believing in yourself
   and the business you're in

Hustle is the sheer joy of winning

Hustle is being the sorest loser in town

Hustle is hating to take a vacation because you
   might miss a piece of the action

Hustle is heaven if you're a hustler

Hustle is hell if you're not

Wesley's Questions

Members of John Wesley's Holy Club, over 200 years ago, asked themselves 22 questions each day in their private devotions.

1. Am I consciously or unconsciously creating the impression that I am a better person than I really am? In other words, am I a hypocrite?
2. Am I honest in all my acts and words, or do I exaggerate?
3. Do I confidentially pass on what was told to me in confidence?
4. Can I be trusted?
5. Am I a slave to dress, friends, work or habit?
6. Am I self-conscious, self pitying, or self-justifying?
7. Did the Bible live in me today?
8. Do I give time to speak to me everyday?
9. Am I enjoying prayer?
10. When did I last speak to someone else of my faith?
11. Do I pray about the money I spend?
12. Do I get to bed on time and get up on time?
13. Do I disobey God in anything?
14. Do I insist on doing something about which my conscience is uneasy?
15. Am I defeated in any part of my life?
16. Am I jealous, impure, irritable, touchy, or distrustful?
17. How do I spend my spare time?
18. Am I proud?
19. Do I thank God I am not as other people, especially as the Pharisees who despised the publican?
20. Is there anyone I fear, or dislike, or criticize, or resent? If so, what am I doing about it?
21. Do I grumble and complain constantly?
22. Is Christ real to me?

BEYOND THE BOUNDS

Lock him in a prison cell... and you have John Bunyan.

Bury him in the snows of Valley Forge... and you have George Washington.

Raise him in abject poverty... and you have Abraham Lincoln.

Strike him down with infantile paralysis... and you have Franklin D. Roosevelt.

Rate him as "mediocre" in chemistry... and you have Louis Pasteur.

Label him "too stupid to learn"... and you have Thomas Edison.

Deafen a genius composer... and you have Ludwig van Beethoven.

Call him a slow learner, retarded and ineducable... and you have Albert Einstein.

Blind him...... and you have Ray Charles
                              George Shearing
                              and Stevie Wonder.

Tell her she's too old to start painting at 80... and you have Grandma Moses.

Call him dull and hopeless and flunk him in the sixth grade...
                              ...and you have Winston Churchill.

Tell a young boy who loves to sketch that he has no talent...
                              ... and you have Walt Disney.

The Commitment of a Servant of Jesus Christ

I am a part of the fellowship of the unashamed
the dye has been cast
I have stepped over the line
the decision has been made.

I won't look back
let up
slow down
back away
or be still.

My past is redeemed
my present makes sense
my future is secure.

I'm finished and done with low living
sight walking
small planning
smooth knees
colorless dreams
tamed visions
mundane talking
cheap giving
and dwarfed goals.

I no longer need pre-eminence
prosperity
position
plaudits
or popularity.

I don't have to be right
first
tops
recognized
praised
regarded
or rewarded.

I now live by faith
lean on His presence
walk in patience
lift by prayer
and labor by power.

The Commitment of a Servant of Jesus Christ...continued.

My face is set
my gait is fast
my goal is heaven
my road is narrow
my way is rough
my companions are few
my guide is reliable
and my mission is clear.

I cannot be bought
compromised
detoured
lured away
turned back
deluded
or delayed.

I will not flinch in the face of sacrifice
hesitate in the presence of adversity
negotiate at the table of the enemy
ponder at the pool of popularity
or meander in the maze of mediocrity.

I won't give up
shut up
or let up until I have stayed up
stored up
prayed up
paid up
and spoken up for the cause of Christ.

I must go until He comes
give until I drop
witness until all know
and work until He stops me.

And when He comes for his own
He will have no problem recognizing me . . .
because my banner will be clear
my scars will be evident
my hope will be realized
and my joy will be full.

It will be worth it all.

I am a committed believer
a dedicated disciple
and a satisfied servant
of the Lord Jesus Christ!

Mohandas K. Gandhi's
List of Seven Deadly Sins

Wealth without work.

Pleasure without conscience.

Knowledge without character.

Business without morality.

Science without humanity.

Politics without principle.

Worship without sacrifice.

Section

Two

Family

HOME QUOTES

A man travels the world over
    in search of what he needs...
        and returns home to find it.   **GEORGE MOORE**

Without a home... there can be no good citizen.
    With a home... there can be no bad one.
                                     ANDREW JOHNSON

Home is the place where,
    when you have to go there,
        they have to take you in.   **ROBERT FROST**

He is happiest,
    be he king or peasant,
        who finds his peace
            in his home.   **JOHANN WOLFAGAN VON GOETHE**

Houses are built to live in...
    not to look on.   **FRANCES BACON**

Where we love is home...
    home that our feet may leave...
        but not our hearts.   **OLIVER WENDELL HOLMES**

WHEN I WAS . . .

4 years old: My Daddy can do anything.

7 years old: My Dad knows a lot, a whole lot.

8 years old: My Father doesn't quite know everything.

12 years old: Oh well, naturally Father doesn't know it all.

14 years old: Father? Hopelessly old-fashioned.

21 years old: Oh, that man is out of date. What did you expect?

25 years old: He knows a little bit about it, but not much.

30 years old: It's amazing how wise he got in the last few years.

35 years old: We need to find out what Dad thinks about it.

50 years old: What would Dad have thought about it.

60 years old: My Dad knew everything.

65 years old: I wish I could talk it over with Dad one more time.

THE HANDS OF MY DAD

When I was just a little guy...
...... they lifted me and cared for me,
...... they were stretched out to reach for me when I tried to take my first step,
...... they guided and directed me and sometimes slapped my wrists,
...... they taught me how to eat waffles and biscuits at the breakfast table, and how to tie my shoes,
...... they took the time to share my play and touch my life with joy,
...... they gently carried me to Church and laid me down to sleep on a hard wood pew,
...... they folded as I learned to pray and then they tucked me into bed.

When I became a boy...
...... they taught me how to hold a baseball bat,
...... they held me when I learned to ride my first bike,
...... they displayed compassion and made a lasting impression upon my life when they reached out to help less fortunate people,
...... they taught me how to play ping pong,
...... they hung decorations on the Christmas tree,
...... they opened the Bible and shared truths that last until today,
...... they covered a saddened face when I selfishly insisted on my own way,
...... they lovingly settled on my shoulders when I was sad and thought nobody cared.

When I became a man...
...... they wiped away my Mother's tears when I went away to college,
...... they caressed mementos of close hours we had shared,
...... they expressed pride as they congratulated me when I graduated,
...... they manifested the love of God by their gentle manner and warmhearted touch.

And today, more than ever...
...... they hold a store of memories that could fill myriad books,
...... they still reach out for a rose... and they still find a four leaf clover,
...... they reach out in tender love... and in their silence, speak volumes,
...... and they still fold themselves in prayer and open friendship's door.

Lessons From My Dad

1. A man's main job is to take care of the people who depend on him.

2. Never boast, never pretend, never say anything that isn't true.

3. Share with the less fortunate.

4. When you say you're going to do something, do it.

5. When you're right, don't quit.

6. Don't turn your back on friends who are down and out.

7. It does no good to complain.

8. Talk with your children.

9. When the grass is greener on the other side of the fence, it's time to fertilize your lawn.

10. When you see a turtle on a fence post, you know he didn't get there by himself.

WHAT IS A GRANDMOTHER?

By Sally Martin, Third Grade

A Grandmother is a lady who has no children of her own.

She likes other people's little girls and boys.

Grandmothers don't have to do anything except be there.

They're old so they shouldn't play hard or run.

It's enough if they drive us to the market where the pretend horse is and have lots of quarters ready.

Or if they take us for walk, they should slow down past things like pretty leaves and caterpillars.

They never say hurry up.

Grandmothers are usually fat, but not too fat to tie your shoe.

They wear glasses and funny underwear.
They can take their teeth and gums off.

Grandmothers don't have to be smart; only answer questions like why isn't God married, and why do dogs chase cats.

Everybody should try to have a Grandmother, especially if you can't watch television, because they are the only grown ups who have time.

The World's Toughest Job Description

It is, without a doubt, the most creative job in the world.

It involves taste,
fashion,
decorating,
recreation,
education,
transportation,
psychology,
romance,
cuisine,
designing,
literature,
medicine
handicraft,
art,
horticulture,
economics,
government,
community relations,
pediatrics,
geriatrics,
entertainment,
maintenance,
purchasing,
direct mail,
law,
accounting,
religion,
energy
and management.

Anybody who handles all that has to be somebody special.

She is.

She's a mother.

A Mother's Rules

Susannah Wesley had 19 children, including John and Charles, the founders of the Methodist Church. The following is the set of rules she strictly enforced. It's an insight into why those children turned out so well.

1. Allow no eating between meals.

2. Put all children in bed by 8:00.

3. Require them to take medicine without complaining.

4. Subdue self-will in a child.

5. Teach each one to pray as soon as he can speak.

6. Require all to be still during family worship.

7. Give them nothing that they cry for, and only that which they ask for politely.

8. To prevent lying, punish no fault which is first confessed and repented of.

9. Never let a sinful act go unpunished.

10. Never punish a child twice for a single offense.

11. Commend and reward good behavior.

12. Any attempt to please, even if poorly performed, should be commended.

13. Preserve property rights, even in the smallest matters.

14. Strictly observe all promises.

15. Require no child to work before he can read well.

16. Teach children to fear the rod.

ALL THE THINGS THEY ARE

A mother is what makes you put on a sweater when she feels cold.

A mother makes you eat spinach 'cause it'll give you good, strong teeth. (She ought to feed it to Grandpa!)

Mother's like the bony pieces of chicken, the burnt pieces of toast, and the smallest pieces of cake.

They like to hoe the longest row and carry the heaviest load.

They know all about things like sugar cookies, band-aids, puppies, Christmas wishes, and broken hearts.

They fix toys that will not run and noses that will not stop.

Mothers write on the hearts of their children things the world will never erase.

The wise mother lets the father wear the pants in the family. She just provides the suspenders.

It's a mother's privilege to have children, her right to love them and her duty to let them go. Have them, love them, let them go. The last, they say, is the hardest of all.

If Mothers Only Knew

MRS. WRIGHT: Orville and Wilbur, you'll never get that bicycle shop off the ground.

MRS. FULTON: Robert, what's got you all steamed up.

MRS. FRANKLIN: Ben, go fly a kite.

MRS MORSE: Sam, stop tapping your fingers on the table . . . you're driving me crazy!

MRS. LINDBERGH: Charles, can't you do anything by yourself?

MRS. WASHINGTON: George never did have a head for money.

MRS. ARMSTRONG: Neil has no more business taking flying lessons than the man in the moon!

TEN COMMANDMENTS
for Self Esteem

1 .SPEND "QUALITY TIME" EACH DAY WITH YOUR CHILDREN. This is an opportunity to hear what they did and what is on their minds.

2. MAKE POSITIVE STATEMENTS TO YOUR CHILDREN AS OFTEN AS POSSIBLE. No one has enough armor to withstand a constant barrage of no and don't.

3. WHEN DISAGREEMENTS OCCUR, ARGUE ONLY ABOUT INACCURATE FACTS OR STATEMENTS. Remember, everyone has opinions. Sometimes we must agree that we disagree.

4. REACH OUT AND TOUCH. Everyone needs it! Everyone wants it! Atouch will communicate much more than just words.

5. SMILE! Be happy around your children.

6. ALLOW CHILDREN TO DEVELOP RESPONSIBILITY. Basically, in order to be a responsible family member, one must have responsibility.

7. BE HONEST WITH YOUR CHILDREN. Children will undoubtedly learn their response patterns from parents. Honesty also shows children you trust them.

8. SEPARATE THE BEHAVIOR FROM THE INDIVIDUAL. In problem situations, make certain the child knows that the behavior, not the child, is unacceptable.

9. DEAL WITH HERE-AND-NOW ISSUES. Dredging up the past may serve to further block communication within the family.

10. WORK ON YOUR OWN POSITIVE SELF-ESTEEM. Happy, well-adjusted human beings who genuinely care for others make excellent parents.

A Manifesto from Your Child

1. **Don't spoil me.**
    > I know quite well I ought not to have all I ask for.
    > I'm only testing you.

2. **Don't be afraid to be firm with me.**
    > I prefer it.
    > It makes me feel more secure.

3. **Don't let me form bad habits.**
    > I have to rely on you to sense them in the early stages.

4. **Don't make me feel smaller than I am.**
    > It only makes me behave stupidly "big".

5. **Don't correct me in front of people if you can help it.**
    > I'll take much more notice if you talk to me privately.

6. **Don't make me feel that my mistakes are sins.**
    > It upsets my sense of values.

7. **Don't be too upset when I say, "I hate you."**
    > It isn't you I hate.
    > It's your power to thwart me.

8. **Don't protect me from consequences.**
    > I need to learn the painful way sometimes.

9. **Don't take too much notice of my small ailments.**
    > Sometimes they get me the attention I need.

10. **Don't nag.**
    > If you do, I shall protect myself by appearing deaf.

11. **Don't make rash promises.**
    > Remember that I feel let down when promises are broken.

(A Manifesto... Continued)

12. **Don't forget I cannot explain myself as well as I would like.**
I'm not always as articulate as you.

13. **Don't tax my honesty too much.**
I am easily frightened into telling lies.

14 **Don't be inconsistent.**
That confuses me and makes me lose faith in you.

15. **Don't put me off when I ask questions.**
If you do, you will find that I stop asking and seek my information elsewhere.

16. **Don't tell me my fears are silly.**
They may be to you but they are terribly real to me, and you can do much to reassure me if you try to understand.

17. **Don't ever suggest that you are perfect or infallible.**
It gives me too great a shock to discover you are neither.

18. **Don't ever think that it is beneath your dignity or position to apologize to me.**
An honest apology makes me feel very warm toward you.

19. **Don't forget that I love experimenting.**
I couldn't get along without it, so please put up with it.

20. **Don't forget how quickly I am growing up.**
It must be very difficult for you to keep pace with me.
But please try.

21. **Don't forget that to thrive I need lots of understanding love.**
But I guess I don't need to tell you that, do I?

KID'S EYE VIEW OF MARRIAGE

WHAT IS MARRIAGE ALL ABOUT?

Marriage is when you get to keep your girl and don't have to give her back to her parents!

Marriage means spending a lot of time together... even if you don't want to!

It's when two people who have a house and kids decided to take the same name so that other people don't get confused.

HOW DO YOU DECIDE WHOM TO MARRY?

You flip a nickel and heads means you stay with him and tails means you try the next one.

You talk about life while you eat cheeseburgers and make believe that you aren't looking at each other's figures!

To figure out who you should marry, you have to close your eyes and let a bunch of them kiss you until one of them makes you see stars... He's the lucky guy!

HOW DO YOU MAKE MARRIAGE WORK?

Have a lot of kids. Even if you have fights, you'll stick it out for the kid's sake... unless they're brats.

Wear a lot of sexy clothes... like underwear that is red and has a few diamonds on it.

Tell your wife that she looks pretty even if she looks like a truck!

WHAT PROMISES DO PEOPLE MAKE WHEN THEY GET MARRIED?

To go through sickness, illness and diseases together.

To share the TV and not argue when she wants to watch a romantic movie and he wants to watch football games.

The bride promises that they're going to have a lot of love and be obedient to each other, and the groom mostly just looks at his watch because he's always sweating and wants to get out of there.

The Animal I'd Like To Be

School children in Orlando Elementary Schools were asked what kind of animal they would choose to be. Here are the best answers:

THERESA SCHMID, Age 9
I would be a tyrannosaurus rex so I could eat my 11-year-old brother. He wouldn't taste too good, but it would be worth it to get rid of him. He's a pain in the neck.

BONNIE COINS, Age 8
I'd be a kangaroo so if my mother started chasing me to spank me, I could get away from her. Being able to jump high would make it easier to clean the paddle fans, too.

BRIAN FICK, Age 8
I'd like to be a lion so I could tell my parents when to go to bed and I could stay up as late as I wanted. But not having to take a bath would be the best part. If I smelled bad, it wouldn't matter... everyone would be too scared to complain.

BILLY PARKER, Age 8
I'd be a blue jay so if somebody below was wearing a wig, I could swoop down and take it off with my claws. That would be pretty funny. I'd start with my friend's dad.

ONEIDA WHITE, Age 9
I'd be a giraffe so I could wear hundreds of necklaces.

KATRINA GRBIC, Age 9
I would be a cheetah so my mother would quit being worried about me wanting to go out with boys. Human moms worry about that kind of thing. Cheetah moms don't.

SHENITA JONES, Age 9
I'd like to be an ant because it's better than being an uncle.

Historic Hysteria

Moses went up Mount Cyanide to get the Ten Commandments.

King Solomon had 300 wives and 700 porcupines.

William Tell shot an arrow through an apple while standing on his son's head.

The climate of the Sahara Desert is so hot that the inhabitants have to live someplace else.

Queen Elizabeth exposed herself before her troops and they all shouted, "Hurrah!"... then her navy went out and defeated the Spanish Armadillo.

Benjamin Franklin invented electricity by rubbing two cats backward.

Abraham Lincoln was born in a log cabin which he built with his own hands. He got shot by John Wilkes Booth, one of the actors in a play. This ruined Booth's career!

A virgin forest is a forest in which the hand of man has never set foot.

The general direction of the Alps is straight up.

The spinal column is a long bunch of bones. The head sits on top and you sit on the bottom.

One of the major functions of skin is to keep people who look at you from throwing up.

Joan of Ark was Noah's wife.

The fifth commandment is: Humor thy father and mother.

Paraffin is next in order after seraphim.

The patron saint of travelers is St. Francis of the sea sick.

One of the main causes of dust is janitors.

Oliver Cromwell had a large, red nose, but under it were deeply religious feelings.

In the middle of the 18th century all the morons moved to Utah.

IF A CHILD LIVES WITH...

If a child lives with criticism .... he learns to condemn.

If a child lives with hostility .... he learns to fight.

If a child lives with ridicule .... he learns to be shy.

If a child lives with shame .... he learns to feel guilty.

If a child lives with tolerance .... he learns to be patient.

If a child lives with praise .... he learns appreciation.

If a child lives with fairness.... he learns to show equality.

If a child lives with security .... he learns to have faith.

If a child lives with acceptance .... he learns to find love.

ACTUAL SCHOOL EXCUSES

Dear School: Please accuse John from being absent on January 29, 30, 31, 32 and 33.

Please execute Johnny for being. It was his father's fault.

Mary could not come to school because she was bothered by very close veins.

Lillie was absent from school yesterday because she had a going over.

Please excuse Joyce from P.E. for a few days. Yesterday she fell off a tree and misplaced her hip.

Sorry Joey wasn't in Spanish class yesterday. His throat was so sore he could hardly speak English.

The reason Charlie was late today is that we are a family of two working parents, four children and one bathroom.

Please excise Ray Friday from school. He has very loose vowels.

Marianne was absent December 11-16 because she had a fever, sore throat, headache, and upset stomach. Her sister was also sick (fever and sore throat) and her brother had a low grade fever and ached all over. I wasn't the best either (sore throat and fever). There must be the flu going around, her father even got hot last night.

Please excuse Sarah for being absent. She was sick and I had her shot.

THROUGH THE YEARS

SITUATION #1
The husband says, "I sure do like ladies with long hair!"

FIRST YEAR RESPONSE   She lets her hair grow.
FIFTH YEAR RESPONSE   She lets her daughter's hair grow.
TENTH YEAR RESPONSE   She asks, "What happened to your hair?"

SITUATION #2
The wife sees a beautiful coat in the department store window
and she just has to have it!

FIRST YEAR RESPONSE   She works Saturdays to earn extra money.
FIFTH YEAR RESPONSE   She learns to live without it
TENTH YEAR RESPONSE   She buys the coat . . . for her daughter.

SITUATION #3
Her Mother just called . . . again . . . and said,
"I haven't seen you in a long time."

FIRST YEAR RESPONSE   You invite Mother for a week and you both sleep
on the lumpy studio couch.
FIFTH YEAR RESPONSE   Mother sleeps on the lumpy studio couch.
TENTH YEAR RESPONSE   You send the children home to Mother.

SITUATION #4
The husband says, "I like my shirts with no starch."

FIRST YEAR RESPONSE   The wife does not put starch in the wash.
FIFTH YEAR RESPONSE   She tells the laundry . . ."No starch!"
TENTH YEAR RESPONSE   She says, "Look, Charlie! Just be glad the shirts
are clean."

SITUATION #5
The husband comes home from work cranky, irritable and tired.

FIRST YEAR RESPONSE   She kisses him and says . . .
"I'm glad you're home. I love you."
FIFTH YEAR RESPONSE   She kisses him and says . . .
"I'm glad you're home. I love you."
TENTH YEAR RESPONSE   She kisses him and says . . .
"I'm glad you're home. I love you."

And that's what marriage is all about . . . to love and be loved.

Resolutions for the Improvement of Relationships

Since one's perception of oneself is not always perfectly clear, it is my belief that resolutions are best made by one for another. In other words, I define resolutions for your flaws and weaknesses, and you define mine.

With that in mind, I polled a few friends for resolutions relating to the opposite sex. Men suggest those for wives and vice versa. You might say these are consensus resolutions... generalizations with an intentionally sexist bent.

Ladies first... please.

1. **DO NOT UNDER ANY CIRCUMSTANCES,** under any influences, for any reason whatsoever discuss gynecological practices, issues, phobias, processes, recollections or reflections in the presence of men.

2. **DO NOT EXAGGERATE** the value (sacrifice, strain, burden) of raising children/keeping a house/giving a party.

3. **DO NOT TELL MEN MORE THAN ONCE** that they have no idea how hard it is being a woman.

4. **DO NOT FEEL COMPELLED AT AGE 40** to begin looking like your mother.

5. **DO PRETEND YOU ARE STILL DATING** and that it's important to look good.

6. **DO CLOSE THE DOOR** to the bathroom.

7. **DO ALLOW HIM TO FEEL** that he is stronger (and sometimes smarter) than you are... even if it isn't true.

8. **DO REMEMBER ALL THE NICE THINGS MOTHERS SAY** to their little boys and repeat them. More or less.

9. **DO NOT CHARGE** his birthday present on his own Mastercard. Use his Visa.

10. **DO BE AFFECTIONATELY AGGRESSIVE** more than once a year.

11. **DO THROW OUT YOUR OLD UNDERWEAR** the instant you wonder if you should.

12. **DO PICK UP THE CHECK** every now and then, even if he is your husband.

13. **DO TRY TO REMEMBER**, at least once a day, why you liked him in the first place.

Resolutions for the Improvement of Relationships.. Continued

And now gentlemen, it's your turn. Pretty please.

1. **DO NOT EXPECT A PURPLE HEART** every time you take out the garbage.

2. **DO NOT PUT THE DISHES** in the dishwasher and then claim you've cleaned the kitchen. The kitchen isn't clean until the counters are wiped and the floor is swept.

3. **DO NOT EXAGGERATE** the value (sacrifice, strain, burden) of Going to Work.

4. **DO NOT TELL** women that labor pains don't really hurt.

5. **DO NOTICE** when your wife changes her hairstyle.

6. **DO NOT TELL THE TRUTH** if you do not like her new hairstyle.

7. **DO PRETEND YOU'RE STILL DATING** and that a large girth will hinder your romantic efforts.

8. **DO REMEMBER** birthday, anniversaries and Valentine's Day.

9. **DO NOT BELIEVE HER** when she says she does not want anything for her birthday, anniversary or Valentines Day.

10. **DO SEND FLOWERS.** Any time.

11. **DO CALL HOME** when you're running late. No, she's not your Mother, but she may have a romantic dinner planned.

12. **DO THROW OUT YOUR OLD UNDERWEAR** before she has to.

13. **DO TRY TO REMEMBER,** at least once a day, why you liked her in the first place.

SECTION THREE

Humor

Murphy's Laws...

AND OTHER TRUTHS

Anything that can go wrong, will go wrong.

No good deed goes unpunished.
Leakproof seals will.
Self-starters will not.
Interchangeable parts won't.

There is always one more problem.

If you're feeling good, don't worry... you'll get over it.

All warranties expire upon payment of invoice.

Never eat prunes when you are famished.

Friends come and go... but enemies accumulate.

If you try to please everybody, nobody will like it.

A short cut is the longest distance between two points.

You will always find something in the last place you look, because when you find it, you stop looking.

Every solution breeds new problems.

It is impossible to make anything foolproof because fools are so ingenious.

The race is not always to the swift nor the battle to the strong, but that is the way to bet.

When in doubt, mumble. When in trouble, delegate.

There's never time to do it right, but there's always time to do it over.

Everything east of the San Andreas Fault will eventually plunge into the Atlantic Ocean.

Nature always sides with the hidden flaw.

A bird in the hand is safer than two overhead.

Celibacy is not hereditary.

Murphy's Laws...
AND OTHER TRUTHS {Continued}

Beauty is only skin deep. Ugly goes to the bone.

The chance of a piece of bread falling with the buttered side down is directly proportional to the cost of the carpet.

The other line always moves faster.

A $300.00 picture tube will protect a 10 cent fuse by blowing first.

If it jams, force it. If it breaks, it needed replacing anyway.

Nothing is impossible for the man who doesn't have to do it.

Any tool dropped while repairing a car will roll underneath to the exact center.

The repairman will never have seen a model quite like yours before.

When a broken appliance is demonstrated for the repairman, it will automatically work perfectly.

Never eat yellow snow.

Everyone has a scheme for getting rich that will not work.

If everything seems to be going well, you obviously don't know what is going on.

If more than one person is responsible for a miscalculation, no one will be at fault.

Early to bed and early to rise makes a man... a father.

Never argue with a fool. People might not know the difference.

Nothing is as easy as it looks.

A penny saved is not worth very much.

Living well is the best revenge.

WHAT'S IN A NAME...
NOT MUCH!

A rose is a rose... but a jackrabbit isn't a rabbit, it's a hare... and a guinea pig isn't from New Guinea nor is it a pig, it's a rodent.

The Caspian Sea is also misnamed. It's not really a sea... it's the world's largest lake.

The firefly isn't a fly, it's a beetle.

The name catgut is hogwash... the material is made from the intestines of sheep and other animals... never cats.

A horned toad isn't a toad, it's a lizard.

Koala bears aren't bears. The koala is a cousin of the kangaroo.

And your funny bone isn't a bone at all, it's a nerve located at the back of your elbow.

Belonging to a Christian Church does not make you a Christian. That doesn't happen until you believe.

And sitting through a Church Service does not make you a servant. That only comes by doing.

Unfulfilled Prophecies

When it says empty, there are always a few gallons left.

꙳

They'll feel wonderful once you break them in.

꙳

We're bringing it in right under budget.

꙳

You can assemble it yourself in minutes.

꙳

It won't feel cold once you dive in.

꙳

You'll housebreak him in no time.

꙳

What you don't know won't hurt you.

꙳

It doesn't cost anything to look.

The World's **WORST** Predictions

Everything that can be invented has been invented.
> U.S. Patent Office Director urging President McKinley to abolish the office (1899)

I think there is a world market for about five computers.
> Thomas J. Watson, IBM (1958)

The ordinary horseless carriage is a luxury for the wealthy. It will never come into as common use as the bicycle.
> Literary digest (1899)

Any general system of conveying passengers at a velocity exceeding 10 miles per hour is extremely improbable.
> Thomas Tregold, British railroad designer (1835)

The population of the earth decreases every day. In another 10 centuries the earth will be nothing but a desert.
> Montesquieu, French philosopher (1743)

Atomic energy might be as good as our present-day explosives, but it is unlikely to produce anything very much more dangerous.
> Winston Churchill (1939)

I will ignore all ideas for new works and engines of war, the invention of which has reached its limits, and for whose improvement, I see no further possibility.
> Julius Frontinus, Roman military engineer (1st century A.D.)

The phonograph is not of any commercial value.
> Thomas Edison (1915)

When the Paris Exhibition closes, electric light will close with it, and no more will be heard of it.
> Erasmus Wilson, Oxford University professor (1878)

While theoretically and technically television may be feasible, commercially and financially I consider it an impossibility, a development of which we need waste little time dreaming.
> Lee DeForest, American inventor (1926)

I cannot conceive of anything more ridiculous, more absurd and more affrontive to sober judgment than the cry that we are profiting by and acquisition of New Mexico and California. I hold that they are not worth a dollar.
> U.S. Senator Daniel Webster (1848)

So many centuries after the Creation it is unlikely that anyone could find hitherto unknown lands of any value.
> A report to King Ferdinand and Queen Isabella of Spain (1486)

TRASH TO Treasure

Wacky donations received by the Salvation Army in Portland, Oregon... and they've been able to sell most of it!

An entire truckload of like-new furniture and appliances... donated in a fit of anger by a man getting a divorce from his wife.

But turn about is fair play... so the next morning the soon-to-be-ex-wife showed up at the store and donated all her hubby's clothes!

A farmer contributed the stuffed head of his prize goat, apparently because he couldn't stand to look at his deceased pal. A Salvation Army worker mounted the head and it sold the next day.

Another store received a box containing the ashes of an Indian tribal leader!

A dog owner gave his pooch's baby teeth, which at least had sentimental value... if nothing else.

Another pet owner donated a dry aquarium containing the withered remains of several tropical fish.

Still another store received two buckets of fish bait, but it was useless because they'd been preserved in formaldehyde. But the store sold the buckets... after they'd been cleansed of the bait.

They have received a collection of live garter snakes and a World War I French machine gun.

And a retiring clown donated two of his old outfits, including his floppy shoes, the big red nose... and a lapel flower that squirts water.

THEATRICAL LOGIC

In is down, down is front;
out is up, up is back.

Off is out, on is in;
right is left and left is right.

A drop shouldn't
and
a block and fall does neither.

A prop doesn't
and
a cove has no water.

Tripping is OK.

A running crew rarely gets anywhere.

A purchase line will get you nothing.

A drop will not catch anything,
and
a gridiron has nothing to do with football.

Strike is work (and a lot of it),
and
a green room, thank God, isn't.

Now that you're fully versed in theatrical terms
"BREAK A LEG..."

But not really.

BUMPER SNICKERS

DO NOT WASH
Vehicle undergoing scientific dirt test

FORTY ISN'T OLD
if you're a tree

AS A MATTER OF FACT
I do own the road

GOOD PLANETS ARE HARD TO FIND

MY BOSS IS A JEWISH CARPENTER

LIFE IS UNCERTAIN
eat dessert first

WHEN THE GOING GETS TOUGH
it's time to take a nap

MY HUSBAND IS LIVING PROOF
that women can take a joke

I'VE BEEN DIETING FOR A WEEK
and all I've lost is seven days

I'VE USED UP ALL MY SICK DAYS
so I'm calling in dead

I'M TRYING TO LOSE WEIGHT
but it keeps finding me

IF AT FIRST YOU DON'T SUCCEED,
do it the way your wife told you to

IF MAMA AIN'T HAPPY
ain't nobody happy

Insurance Excuses

Actual summaries submitted when automobile insurance policy-holders were asked for a brief statement describing their particular accident.

The other car collided with mine without giving any warning of its intention.

A pedestrian hit me and went under my car.

The guy was all over the road. I had to swerve a number of times before I hit him.

I pulled away from the side of the road, glanced at my mother-in-law and headed over the embankment.

The accident occurred when I was attempting to bring my car out of a skid by steering it into the other vehicle.

I was driving my car out of the driveway in the usual manner, when it was struck by the other car in the same place it had been struck several times before.

I was on my way to the doctor's with rear end trouble when my universal joint gave way, causing me to have an accident.

As I approached the intersection, a stop sign suddenly appeared in a place where no stop sign had ever appeared before. I was unable to stop in time to avoid the accident.

The telephone pole was approaching fast. I was attempting to swerve out of its path when it struck my front end.

Insurance Excuses... {Continued}

To avoid hitting the bumper of the car in front of me, I struck the pedestrian.

An invisible car came out of nowhere, struck my vehicle and vanished.

The pedestrian had no idea which direction to go, so I ran over him.

I saw a slow-moving, sad-faced old gentleman as he bounced off the hood of my car.

Coming home, I drove into the wrong house and collided with a tree I don't have.

The indirect cause of this accident was a little guy in a small car with a big mouth.

I had been shopping for plants all day and was on my way home. As I reached an intersection, a hedge sprung up, obscuring my vision.

My car was legally parked as it backed into the other vehicle.

I drove my truck under a bridge, and it didn't fit.

You Know You're Really From Alabama If...

..... your richest relative buys a new house and you have to help take off the wheels.

..... you think Spam on a saltine is an hors d'oeuvre.

..... there is a stuffed possum mounted anywhere in your home.

..... you consider iced tea and a bug zapper quality entertainment.

..... less than half the cars you own run.

..... the primary color of your car is Bond-O.

..... directions to your house include "turn off the paved road."

..... your family tree does not fork.

..... your brother-in-law is also your uncle.

..... you have refused to watch the Academy Awards ever since SMOKEY AND THE BANDIT was snubbed for Best Picture.

..... the rear tires of your car are twice as wide as the front ones.

..... you prominently display a gift you bought at Graceland.

..... you consider OUTDOOR LIFE deep reading.

..... the diploma hanging in your den includes the words, "Trucking Institute".

..... your mother keeps a spit cup on the ironing board.

You Know You're Really From Alabama If ...Continued

..... you think beef jerky and moon pies are two of the basic food groups.

..... you've ever worn a tube top to a wedding.

..... you think Campho Phenique is a miracle drug.

..... you have more than two brothers named Bubba and Junior.

..... Your father encouraged you to quit school because Larry had an opening on the lube rack.

..... you think the styrofoam cooler is the greatest invention of all time.

..... you have a rag for a gas cap.

..... you had a toothpick in your mouth when your wedding pictures were taken.

..... your lifetime goal is to own a fireworks stand.

..... your Dad walks you to school because you're both in the same grade.

..... your house doesn't have curtains, but your truck does.

..... your Junior-Senior Prom had day care.

..... you need one more hole punched in your card to get a freebie at House of Tattoos.

..... you think the Space Program is fake... but wrestling is real.

RULES OF THUMB

A rule of thumb is a shot in the dark tempered by experience, judgment and raw ingenuity... and it's as good as any other rule we live by. Sometimes better. Like these . . .

People touring attractions, such as Walt Disney World, are more likely to turn to the right. Therefore, the exhibits to the left are less crowded.

Let a strange dog sniff the back of your closed hand. Don't show him your fingers... they're easier to bite.

The more buttons fastened on a person's shirt, the higher the I.Q.

Walking is faster than waiting for a bus, if you're going less than a mile.

You can mail five sheets of paper with a 29-cent stamp.

A man's waist measurement should not exceed his hip measurement. A woman's waist measurement should be less than 80% of her hip measurement.

The distance from your elbow to your wrist equals the length of your foot.

If someone says, "It's not the money, it's the principle," ... it's the money.

The best lawyer is the one who teaches about your problem. Call a nearby law school and ask who teaches a course in the specialty you need. Then find out whether he practices privately.

Ninety percent of bad checks carry numbers below 150, indicating a new account.

The average time between throwing something away and needing it desperately is about two weeks.

The best time to buy a new car is at the end of the month, because the sales people want their monthly reports to look good.

Don't go to a restaurant that has a sign in the window advertising for waiters. It's hard enough to get waited on in a restaurant that thinks it has plenty of help.

A rule of thumb (including this one) works four out of five times.

Rules That Explain Almost Everything

The laws that regulate our universe are mysterious, and mostly beyond our understanding. But there are a number of not-quite-scientific principles that address the ironies and frustrations of everyday life. These are a blend of folk wisdom and management theory... a useful guide as we look toward the 21st century.

BUSINESS Every new project goes through three phases:
1. It will not work.
2. It will cost too much.
3. I thought it was a good idea all along.

CHILDREN If you don't want your children to hear what you are saying, pretend you're talking to them.

DINING In every restaurant, the hardness of the butter pats increases in direct proportion to the softness of the bread being served.

DRIVING The more decrepit the vehicle, the more maniacal the driver.

ECONOMICS You do not want the one you can afford.

The more the name of a product promises, the less it delivers. (For instance, a cheap stereo often has the word "super" in its name.)

Nothing gives a used car more miles per gallon than the salesman.

MARRIAGE The only union that cannot be organized. Both sides think they are management.

PROBABILITY The farther a theater seat is from the aisle, the later the patron arrives.

The smallest hole will eventually empty the large container, unless it is made intentionally for drainage, in which case it will clog.

If it wasn't for the last minute, nothing would get done.

POLITICS Any country with "democratic" in the title isn't.

PROPER WEIGHT CONTROL AND PHYSICAL FITNESS

Many people who are engaged in sedentary occupations do not realize that calories can be burned by the hundreds in strenuous activities that do not require physical exercise. Here is the simple guide to calorie-burning exertion and the number of calories per hour they consume:

Putting all your eggs in one basket	80
Getting your ducks in a row	150
Beating around the bush	75
Jumping to conclusions	100
Climbing the walls	150
Swallowing your pride	50
Passing the buck	25
Throwing your weight around (depending on your weight)	50-300
Dragging your heels	100
Pushing your luck	250
Making mountains out of molehills	500
Hitting the nail on the head	50
Bending over backwards	75
Jumping on the bandwagon	200
Running around in circles	350
Eating crow	225
Tooting your own horn	25
Climbing the ladder of success	750
Pulling out all the stops	75
Adding fuel to the fire	150
Opening a can of worms	50
Shooting the bull	660

Conversation Between Two Georgia Fishermen

Hiyamac.

Lobuddy.

Benearlong?

Cuplours.

Ketchaneny?

Goddafew.

Kindrthey?

Basanacarp.

Ennysiztuem?

Cupplapounz.

Hittinhard?

Sordalite.

Wachauzin?

Dobbawurms.

Fishonahboddum?

Rydonnahboddum.

Igoddago.

Tubad.

Seeyaroun.

Yatakidezy.

Guluk.

DO'S AND DON'TS FOR DUFFERS

1. No heckling of other golfers when they are about to hit, unless you heard them snicker at you at your last hit, or unless you are down by at least 5 strokes.

2. It is improper for you, while your competitor is preparing to swing, to sit in the cart flipping the reverse gear thereby causing a disturbing "beep".

3. It is acceptable to move your ball within the fairway if you determine that they did a really lousy job cutting the grass. The most logical place for your ball is on top of an ant hill.

4. It is proper to yell, "FORE," when you have hit a ball in the direction of other golfers. It is recommended that you yell prior to the landing of the ball. Other terms deemed unacceptable are, "FIVE," "NINE," and "GOTCHA."

5. When tending a flagstick, you should always do your best to position the flag nearest the center of the hole.

6. It is improper to walk over the ground between your opponents ball and the hole. However, if it seems crowded on the green, you may have no alternatives.

7. The water stations along the course are there for quenching thirst. It is improper to use the containers to mix Koolaid to satisfy your own personal sweet tooth. However, an occasional lemon twist adds a tint of flavor.

8. It is quite normal to lose your scorecard somewhere along the 17th or 18th hole after an especially difficult round. Golfers have also been known to lose pencils around the 15th and 16th hole. However, when you have had an especially good round, everyone will understand if you inadvertently leave your card laying out on the table at the 19th hole.

When the Cure was Worse than the Care

Primitive medicine men tried to scare disease-causing spirits out of patients by beating drums wildly and screaming at them.

Ancient Babylonians believed a patient's symptoms could be transferred to a sheep by breathing into the animal's nostrils.

In medieval times, sore feet were bathed in fresh blood.

Just before the beginning of the Renaissance in Italy, spider bites from tarantulas were treated with music and wild dancing. People danced to the fast music for hours until they felt better. That dance, called the tarantella, is still danced today.

In the 1800s people who had drowned were rubbed with salt. It was thought the salt would draw water out of the person.

Baldness was treated by rubbing the head with onions until the scalp was red, then rubbing it with honey.

Cysts were covered with an ointment made by baking a live bull frog in butter.

Persons suffering from parasitic worms were instructed to take a tablespoon of molasses, mix it with a teaspoon of rust from tin and then drink it.

Before the use of aspirin, childhood fevers were nursed by mixing rattlesnake venom and sweet palm tea and then feeding it to the child once an hour until the fever dropped.

A cure for indigestion that sounds worse than the ailment was to swallow six gravel stones the size of a pea from a cool brook every morning for nine days. Then burn beef bones, grind them fine and eat a spoonful of the powder at every meal.

Even into the early 1900s people tried to cure nosebleeds by leaving rusty nails in cider vinegar and then drinking the liquid.

To remove warts, our ancestors rubbed them with blood from a black-feathered chicken . . . or the hand of a corpse.

Incredibly, some of the bizarre cures worked, like the Babylonian discovery that drinking beer mixed with onion cured sore, dry eyes. The solution made the eyes water.

And Egyptians used moldy bread to cure bacterial infections. They just didn't know that the mold was penicillin.

101 Excuses for Cheating on Your Diet

1. Everybody says fat people are jolly.
2. I'm allergic to health food.
3. I'm addicted to chocolate.
4. Big is beautiful.
5. Thin may be in, but fat is where it's at.
6. Dieting is cruel and unusual punishment.
7. Sugar increases my energy level.
8. Somebody has to keep the dentists in work.
9. If I lose weight my clothes won't fit.
10. My VCR ate my aerobics video.
11. My aerobics record is warped.
12. I don't have time to eat right.
13. Fruits and vegetables carry pesticides.
14. If God had meant for me to eat celery and cottage cheese, He wouldn't have given me taste buds.
15. My Pizza coupons are about to expire.
16. The ice cream shop is on my way home.
17. There's more of me to hug.
18. Dieting makes me grouchy.
19. Fast weight-loss is counter-productive.
20. Because I'm hungry!
21. Deep dish double deluxe frosted fudge brownies.
22. Cherry cheesecake.
23. Pizza.
24. Somebody made me a cake... and I don't want to hurt their feelings.
25. Dieting is not one of the Ten Commandments.
26. My stomach is growling so loud I can't hear myself think.
27. My cheating makes other fat people feel better.
28. I read that it is better to eat six meals a day.
29. I don't want to make other people jealous.
30. There are so may diets I don't know which one to choose.
31. The holidays are coming.
32. Artificial sweeteners aren't good for you.
33. My dog ate my calorie counter guide.
34. The spring on my scale broke.

35. My cat ate the last can of tuna fish.
36. My panty hose stay up better.
37. My Mom taught me to always clean my plate.
38. If nobody sees me eat it, the calories don't count.
39. I never start a diet on days that end in "y".
40. Because I'm hungry.
41. It's good for the economy.
42. The latest fad diet hasn't hit the tabloids yet.
43. I'm bored.
44. I'm depressed.
45. I'm happy.
46. I'm sad.
47. I'm being attacked by the munchies.
48. The four basic food groups are: cakes, pies, candy and pastries.
49. A lot of famous people are fat.
50. Icing is good for my peaches and cream complexion.
51. But I'm drinking diet cola.
52. I can't count my calories because my calculator only goes to 9,999,999.
53. Valentine candy is half price.
54. Easter candy is half price.
55. Halloween candy is half price.
56. Christmas candy is half price.
57. I'm so hungry I could eat my socks.
58. My jaws need exercise.
59. What's a party without junk food.
60. Because I'm hungry!
61. Cake has fiber.
62. Why eat carrots when I can have carrot cake?
63. I can't exercise because muscle weighs more than fat.
64. I always lose weight in the wrong places.
65. Big hips run in my family.
66. I'm not over-weight... I'm just big-boned.
67. I volunteered to be a taste tester for a marketing survey.
68. Everybody puts sugar in everything.

101 Excuses for Cheating... Continued

69. Even the Bible agrees that man can't live by bread alone.
70. When it's time to clean out my refrigerator, I hate to throw anything away.
71. I sleep better on a full stomach.
72. I'm warmer in the winter with a few extra pounds.
73. I'm afraid of becoming anorexic.
74. I can't afford a new wardrobe.
75. Who cares about the swimsuit season, anyway?
76. It's not weight gain, it's water retention.
77. My potato chips will get stale.
78. My ice cream will get freezer burn.
79. My friends are all having birthdays.
80. Because I'm hungry!
81. If I don't eat Aunt Elma's potato salad, who will?
82. Our church is having a pot-luck supper.
83. The ladies Missionary Group is having a bake sale.
84. The Youth Group is selling candy bars.
85. I have to fix it for my family anyway.
86. I have to test this new recipe before I serve it to company.
87. My sister-in-law's cousin's neighbor's best friend said that too much dieting can be bad for you.
88. The spirit is willing, but the flesh is weak.
89. I've already lost 2,487 pounds in my lifetime.
90. I'll just gain it back anyway.
91. My freezer broke and I have to eat up all my frozen doughnuts.
92. I have to buy ice cream to keep my ice cubes from feeling lonely.
93. Healthy food is too expensive.
94. I have a new recipe I'm dying to try out.
95. I don't want to go into sugar withdrawal.
96. I want to use my new dishes.
97. I'm celebrating National Dessert Month.
98. If I lost weight, I'd have to have new pictures taken.
99. I don't want to slow my metabolism.
100. I don't want to be featured in a Before and After picture.
101. Because I'm hungry!

TRIP-UPS

These are the things you hate to hear when traveling:

1. I thought you were listening when he was giving us directions.

2. It isn't on the map.

3. Still glad we took the scenic back roads?

4. Folks, in my 42 years of piloting, I've never seen anything like this.

5. According to your policy, a "masked holdup" is any act of God.

6. I've never seen a rash like that in my life.

7. Didn't you know this is our monsoon season?

8. What reservation?

9. We believe we found part of your suitcase.

10. Here are some candles and matches.

11. This is not your passport.

12. In your money, that converts to... hold onto your hat.

13. No... the man you gave your bags to does not work here.

14. Hey, Bubba... you'll never guess where these folks think they are.

15. Of course I can hear the boiler room over your phone. Now how may I help you?

DON'T KNOCK KNOCK-KNOCKS

ABBY loving you... always.

ANITA LOOS some weight.

I'll be **DON AMECHE** in a taxi, Honey.

WILL DURANT be paid this month.

AMARYLLIS state agent . . . wanna buy a house?

ARMAGEDDON tired of waiting for you.

FORMALDEHYDE-ing places came the hostile Indians.

AARDVARK a million miles for one of your smiles.

AVONa be alone with you.

MERITRICIOUS and a happy New Year.

ESKIMO, CHRISTIAN, ITALIAN no lies.

TARZAN stripes forever.

DIESEL be your last chance.

It **MARCUS WELBY** spring.

IVY LEAGUE for every drop of rain that falls...

SONY a paper moon.

HONDA the spreading chestnut tree.

MINERVA's wreck from all these knock-knocks.

SECTION

FOUR

Leadership

PARADOXICAL COMMANDMENTS OF LEADERSHIP

1. People are illogical, unreasonable and self-centered.
   Love them anyway.

2. If you do good, people will accuse you of selfish ulterior motives.
   Do good anyway.

3. If you are successful, you win false friends and true enemies.
   Succeed anyway.

4. The good you do today will be forgotten tomorrow.
   Do good anyway.

5. Honesty and frankness make you vulnerable.
   Be honest and frank anyway.

6. The biggest men with the biggest ideas can be shot down by the smallest men with the smallest minds.
   Think big anyway.

7. People favor underdogs but follow only top dogs.
   Fight for a few underdogs anyway.

8. What you spend years building may be destroyed overnight.
   Build anyway.

9. People really need help, but may attack you if you do help them.
   Help them anyway.

10. Give the world the best you have and you'll get kicked in   the teeth.
    Give the world the best you have anyway.

IF BETTER IS POSSIBLE . . . THEN GOOD IS NOT ENOUGH

The Ten Commandments of Leadership

   I. Treat every one with respect and dignity.

   II. Set the example for others to follow.

   III. Be an active coach.

   IV. Maintain the highest standards of honesty and integrity.

   V. Insist on excellence and hold your people accountable.

   VI Build group cohesiveness and pride.

   VII. Show confidence in your people.

   VIII. Maintain a strong sense of urgency.

   IX. Be available and visible to your staff.

   X. Develop yourself to your highest potential.

KNOW THEM

Those who know not
    and know not
       they know not are fools .... shun them.

    Those who know not
       and know
          they know not are learners .... teach them.

        Those who know
          and know not
            they know are asleep .... wake them.

            Those who know
              and know
                they know are wise ...... follow them.

LET'S GET RID OF MANAGEMENT

People don't want to be managed . . . they want to be led.

Whoever heard of a world manager?

World leader, yes.

Educational leader, yes.

Political leader, yes.

Religious leader, yes.

Community leader, yes.

Scout leader, yes.

Labor leader, yes.

Business leader, yes.

But they lead. They don't manage. The carrot always wins over the stick.

Ask your horse. You can lead him to water, but you can't manage him to drink. So you feed him salt to make him thirsty... and that's motivation.

If you want to manage somebody, manage yourself.

Do that well and you'll be ready to stop managing... and start leading.

Section Five

Five

MUSIC

DAFFY-NITIONS

Quotes from Fourth-Grade Essays on Classical Music

Refrain means don't do it. In music it's the part you'd better not sing.

Handel was half German, half Italian and half English. He was rather large.

Beethoven wrote music even though he was deaf. He was so deaf he wrote loud music.

Henry Purcell is a well-known composer only a few people have heard of.

Aaron Copland is a contemporary composer. It is unusual to be contemporary. Most composers do not live until they are dead.

Music sung by two people at the same time is called a duel.

Caruso was at first an Italian. Then someone heard his voice and said he would go a long way. So he came to America.

I know what a sextet is, but I'd rather not say.

HOW'S THAT AGAIN?

God bless America
Thru the night with a light from a bulb!

O Susanna, O don't you cry for me,
For I come from Alabama with a band aid on my knee!

Give us this day our deli bread!

Glory be to the Father
    and to the Son
      and to the Whole East Coast.

We shall come to Joyce's, bringing in the cheese.

Gladly, the consecrated, cross-eyed bear.

He carrots for you.

Bringing in the Sheets.

Yield Not to Penn Station.

Dust Around the Throne.

Praise God from whom all blessings flow,
Praise Him all creatures, HERE WE GO

While the crowd was singing THE STAR SPANGLED BANNER, I noticed the man next to me was speaking the words. When I asked him later why he didn't sing the anthem, he replied, "I've never been able to reach Frances Scott's key."

Olive, the other reindeer, used to laugh and call him names.

"Your car's a mess. What happened?"
"4 calling birds, 3 french hens, 2 turtle doves and a partridge in my pear tree."

Lead on, Oh Kinky Colonel.

While shepherds washed their socks by night.

He socked me and boxed me with His redeeming glove.

𝕳𝕬 𝕳𝕬 IN THREE-QUARTER TIME

Q. How do you get an electric guitar player to turn down the amp?
A. Put a sheet of music in front of him.

Q. What's the definition of a quarter-tone?
A. Two violists playing the same note.

Q. What do you call fifty banjo players at the bottom of the ocean?
A. A good start.

Q. Why are a violist's fingers like lightning?
A. They rarely strike the same spot twice.

Q. What's the difference between a sax and a chain saw?
A. Vibrato.

Q. Why is a violinist like a Scud missile?
A. Both are inaccurate and highly offensive.

Q. How is a bassoon different from an onion?
A. No one cries when you cut up a bassoon.

Q. Define a true gentleman.
A. One who can play the accordion... and doesn't.

Q. What is the range of a viola?
A. About 30 feet... if you kick it far enough.

Q. Why do bagpipers walk around when they play?
A. To get away from the noise.

Q. What do you call 50 violinists buried up to their necks in sand?
A. Not enough sand.

Q. What do violists use for birth control?
A. Their personalities.

Q. What does it mean when viola players drool out of both sides of their mouths?
A. The stage is level.

Q. Why do clarinetists leave their cases on their dashboards?
A. So they can park in handicapped zones.

Q. What's the difference between a bassoon and a trampoline?
A. You take off your shoes before you jump on a trampoline.

Q. Why are violins smaller than violas?
A. They are really the same size. Violinists have larger heads.

Q. What's the difference between a viola and a cello?
A. The cello burns longer.

Q. What's the difference between a soprano and the PLO?
A. You can negotiate with the PLO.

Q. What do you call someone who hangs around with musicians?
A. A drummer.

At a viola convention, the rumor went around that one of the participants could play 32nd notes. Many violists clustered around their colleague and asked him if it was true. He assured everyone it was, so they asked him to prove it and play one.

The drummer and the guitarist were fighting between sets. When asked why, the drummer said the guitarist had thrown his sticks across the room. "He had it coming," blustered the guitarist. "He tuned down one of my strings, and now he won't tell me which one!"

When a musician called a symphony office and asked to speak to the conductor, he was told, "He died." After the first call, the same musician called back 25 times.

"Why do you keep calling and asking the same question?" the receptionist asked.

"I just like to hear you say it," the musician answered.

ONE NIGHT ONLY
THE ALL-STAR BIG BAND AND ORCHESTRA

LEADER - OWEN GUYS

1st Trumpet	Kenny Makit
2nd Trumpet	Diz Astor
3rd Trumpet	Keent Reed
4th Trumpet	Noah Count
Scream Trumpet	Pop Devane
1st Trombone	Hy Registar
2nd Trombone	Slip Shod
3rd Trombone	Willie Show
Bass Trombone	Lew Slips
French Horn	Belle Tone
1st Alto Sax	Otto Tune
2nd Alto Sax	Les Tone
Tenor Sax	Manny Notes
Bari Sax	Ima Growler
1st Violin	Vi Baratto
2nd Violin	Fay Kerr
Viola	Vera Sharp
Cello	Beau Braker
Piano	R. Peggio
Bass	Pete Ziccato
Drums	Phil Dinn
Drums	Chick Boom
Percussion	Perry Diddle
Tuba	Sue Saphone
Vibes	Hal Mallet
Banjo	Ricky Tick
Organ	Page Turner
Asst. Conductor	Justin Case
Arranger	Walt Smedley
Copyist	L. Egible
Librarian	Miss Inga Page
Band Manager	Hiram Cheap
Agent	Gig Booker
Bus Driver	Oliver DaRoad
P.R. Man	Ed Vertise

A CHORISTER'S BEATITUDES

Blessed are the prompt
   for they shall gladden the heart of the director.

Blessed are the enthusiastic
   for they shall move mountains of indifference.

Blessed are the loyal
   for they shall be called the backbone of the choir.

Blessed are those who hunger and thirst for musical knowledge
   for they shall be filled.

Blessed are the peacemakers
   for they shall uplift the spirit of the choir.

Blessed are the humble
   for they shall obtain the respect of their fellow choristers.

Blessed are the diligent
   for they shall see great benefits from their labors.

Blessed are the reverent
   for they shall direct the congregation to God.

Blessed are you when men abuse you and criticize you and utter all
   kinds of evil against you falsely on account of your singing.
   Rejoice and be glad for great is your reward in heaven, for so
   men criticized the singers who were before you.

SPECIAL RULES FOR NEW SINGERS
or
WHY MINISTERS OF MUSIC GET "THAT WAY"

1. When asked to sing in the choir, make sure the veteran members understand that you are doing them a great honor by joining, and be sure that they properly appreciate the superiority of your work over theirs.

2. Never arrive at rehearsals on time. The director has nothing to think about, and it amuses him to guess whether or not you are coming.

3. When order is called for, make as much noise as possible in order to attract the greatest amount of attention. Drop your hymn book, mix up your music, and as soon as the singing has begun, ask which piece is being practiced.

4 Supply the director with a list of your favorite selections; insist on their being used, and never sing in any number which you do not care for. While it is being sung tell the others how ugly it is.

5. Do not wait for the other singers to begin, but assert your independence by always starting ahead of everyone else. This will, of course, annoy the director, but that is what he is there for.

6. Sing the notes correctly... but never mind the words. Remember that it entertains the congregation to guess what you are trying to sing.

7. If the organ has a interlude, occupy it by telling your neighbor what a perfectly awful voice Miss Arpeggio has. If you are not finished when it is time to sing, the organist will be glad to wait for you. If she does not wait, tell her afterwards how perfectly horrid she is.

SPECIAL RULES FOR NEW SINGERS

or

WHY MINISTERS OF MUSIC GET "THAT WAY" ...CONTINUED

8. Do not allow anyone to sing louder than you. Choir rehearsals are held to see who can sing the loudest, and many delightful effects are obtained by each singer trying to prevent anyone else from being heard.

9. Never be satisfied with the starting pitch. If the conductor uses a pitch-pipe, make known your preference for the piano... and vice-versa.

10. Loudly clear your throat during pauses (tenors are trained to do this from birth).

11. Wait until well into a rehearsal before letting the conductor know that you don't have any music.

12. Look at your watch frequently. Shake it in disbelief occasionally.

13. When possible, sing your part either an octave above or below what is written. This is excellent ear-training for the conductor.

14. While the last piece is being sung, put on your wraps and prepare to leave. That is what the last piece is for.

CHOIR PROFICIENCY TEST

In order to measure your level of proficiency as a member of a choral group, the following test has been carefully developed by experts. Read and reflect on each situation and then select the option that will enhance the quality of performance.

1. YOU ARE IN A CHOIR PROCESSIONAL AND SUDDENLY TRIP ON YOUR ROBE AND FALL DOWN. YOU SHOULD...
   ___a. Assume a kneeling position and break into fervent prayer.
   ___b. Pretend that you have had a heart attack.
   ___c. Crawl under the nearest pew.
   ___d. Yell, "I've fallen and I can't get up."

2. YOU ARE A SOPRANO AND COUNT INCORRECTLY. AS A RESULT YOU BOOM OUT A HIGH "C" TOO SOON. YOU SHOULD...
   ___a. Slide into an inspired "O FOR A THOUSAND TONGUES TO SING."
   ___b. Look triumphant and hold that note.
   ___c. Stop abruptly in mid-squawk but keep your lips moving.
   ___d. Sink to the floor in shame.

3. YOU ARE PRESSED INTO EMERGENCY SERVICE CONDUCTING THE CHOIR AND ORCHESTRA IN A VERY IMPORTANT PERFORMANCE WHEN SUDDENLY YOU LOSE YOUR GRIP AND HURL THE BATON INTO THE AUDIENCE. YOU SHOULD...
   ___a. Inform the impaled individual that you have a piece of the rock.
   ___b. Grab the cellist's bow and proceed with aplomb.
   ___c. Without acknowledging the loss, coolly continue and occasionally flex the invisible baton to drive everyone mad.
   ___d. Signal for the house engineer to turn on the lights while you crawl around in search of the lost stick.

CHOIR PROFICIENCY TEST

4. AFTER ALL THOSE LONG, HARD REHEARSALS YOU SHOW UP TWENTY MINUTES LATE FOR THE CONCERT. YOU SHOULD...
   ___a. Climb into the back row of the choir from the baptistry.
   ___b. Read the pamphlet "TECHNIQUES FOR TARDY APPEARANCE" by Justin Case.
   ___c. Slash your wrists in the choir room.
   ___d. Enter pretending that you are the sound technician checking cables and then subtly insinuate yourself into the choir.

5. THE PERSON SHARING YOUR MUSIC AT REHEARSAL HAD A GARLIC TAMALE FOR LUNCH. YOU SHOULD...
   ___a. Complain of lack of air, then grab your throat and fall convulsing to the floor muttering, "Garlic, garlic, garlic."
   ___b. Pass the offender a hymnal opened to "PURIFY ME LORD."
   ___c. Sing without inhaling.
   ___d. Say, "I detect a garlic tamale on your breath. Do you have the recipe for that?"

6. WHILE SINGING THE INVITATIONAL HYMN YOU DISCOVER THAT YOUR HYMNAL HAS THE PAGE MISSING. YOU SHOULD...
   ___a. Hum for your life.
   ___b. Sing, Watermelon, watermelon, watermelon."
   ___c. Improvise an obligato and sing on "OOO."
   ___d. Try to get another hymnal out of the chair rack with your foot.

7. INEVITABLE THAT DREADED BIG SNEEZE COMES TOWARD THE END OF "MAJESTY." YOU SHOULD...
   ___a. As you sneeze, come down hard on your neighbor's instep to create a diversion.
   ___b. Cram your choir robe stole into your mouth to muffle the sound.
   ___c. Try to make the sneeze harmonize.
   ___d. It doesn't really matter because George is going to kill you anyway.

AN HONEST HYMNAL

(If We Sang the Way We Felt)

WHEN MORNING GILDS THE SKIES
MY HEART AWAKENING CRIES
oh no, another day.

AMAZING GRACE HOW SWEET THE SOUND
THAT SAVED A WRETCH LIKE
you.

I LOVE TO TELL THE STORY
have you heard about Jim and Sally?

THE CHURCH'S ONE FOUNDATION
is tax deductible.

I LOVE THY CHURCH, O GOD,
HER WALLS BEFORE ME STAND;
but please excuse my absence, Lord,
my bed feels simply grand!

A CHARGE TO KEEP I HAVE,
A GOD TO GLORIFY;
but Lord, don't ask for cash from me,
that price comes too high.

AM I A SOLDIER OF THE CROSS,
A FOLLOWER OF THE LAMB?
yes! though I seldom pray or pay,
I still insist I am.

MUST JESUS BEAR THE CROSS ALONE,
AND ALL THE WORLD GO FREE?
no! others, Lord, should do their part,
but please don't count on me.

PRAISE GOD FROM WHOM ALL BLESSINGS FLOW,
PRAISE HIM, ALL CREATURES HERE BELOW!
oh, loud my hymns of praise I bring,
because it doesn't cost to sing!

Section
Six
PATRIOTIC

ONE THING IN COMMON

They are, at best, a strange group of men. Yet one unique bond ties them to each other for as long as America records her history.

One was a poor Irish immigrant who died prematurely, leaving a sister to raise his three young sons.

One was so Dutch that English was not spoken in the home.

Another, Scotch-Irish. A farmer who never quite made it big, except in children . . . he fathered nine.

Another was a trader . . . the best he could do for his wife and 11 children was a one-room house for the entire family.

Two were preachers in small churches.

One was a self-appointed doctor . . . he never earned a real medical degree, but took a course by correspondence, and then went from farm to farm offering his questionable services.

Another was a tanner of hides.

Still another . . . a poor laborer who never lived to see the birth of his youngest son.

Missouri was the home of one. He was a mule trader.

Iowa was the state of another. He was a blacksmith.

Tavern-keeper, trolley car conductor, itinerant salesman, frontiersman . . . none really made a mark in a grand or great way.

Mostly ordinary men, in what could be called at best, small professions. But all of these men made it big in one way . . . and it is this that binds these men of two centuries into one special class.

Each one had a son . . .
              who became a President . . .
                          of the United States.

WE NEED HELP

Americans who would change a bad habit	45%
who would change their wealth	64%
who would change their weight	51%
who would change their intelligence	32%
who claim less free time than 3 years ago	90%

Official American work week in 1990	38 hours
in 1910	50 hours

Teenagers with a TV in their bedroom	47%
with a telephone	29%

Average giving per church attender	$701.00
In suburban churches	$895.00
In rural churches	$562.00

Number of employed ministers in U.S. in 1990	350,000
Social workers	540,000
Lawyers and judges	760,000
High school teachers	1,200,000
Secretaries and typists	5,000,00

Teenagers who'd give clergy they know a grade of "A"	52%
"B"	29%
"C"	9%

1990 marriages with at least one partner previously married	50%
In 1970	31%

U.S. children born out of wedlock in 1990	25%
in 1950	4%

SPECIAL LADIES

Of all the women who've lived in the United States... there are forty-two special ladies who fit into one elite category.

Geography has nothing to do with their similarity. Two each came from Tennessee, Iowa, Missouri, New Jersey and Massachusetts.

New York contributed seven ladies and one even came from London, England.

Six called Ohio home and another six claimed Virginia.

Others hailed from North Carolina, Maryland, New Hampshire, Michigan, Kentucky, Pennsylvania, Connecticut, Georgia, Vermont, Nevada and of course, there had to be one from Texas.

Six were widows and three were divorcees.

Ten were ministers' daughters, while others came from educators' homes, poverty stricken farms, or military families, or merchant shops or rough frontier cabins.

They were named Jane and Mary and Betty and Sarah and Edith and Grace. But don't forget Lucretia or Eliza or Letitia or Hannah.

Collectively they mothered 83 sons and 56 daughters.

Some were excellent horsewomen, others fine musicians and outstanding linguists.

You would find some were comfortably hosting lavish parties and receptions, while others were reclusive and withdrew from all crowds and any public attention.

Some eloped or had secret weddings while others had the most elaborate ceremonies imaginable.

So what brought all these forty-five ladies from two centuries together?

Simple... it was love.

They each were the wife of a President of the United States.

WHITE HOUSE FAVORITES

Barbara Bush accepted three cases of broccoli on March 26, 1990 from a fruit and vegetable growers' group, which also shipped 10 tons of the stuff to Washington food banks in response to President Bush's outcry against the vegetable.

But he is far from the only president who had quirks about his food.

HERBERT HOOVER, an orphan, was sent to live with Oregon relatives who made pear butter. He never could face pears again.

FRANKLIN ROOSEVELT was so annoyed by White House food he quipped he ran for a fourth term so he could fire the chef.

HARRY TRUMAN would only eat the end cuts of roast beef.

DWIGHT EISENHOWER loved to cook and had his own secret recipes for beef stew and quail hash.

JOHN KENNEDY, a son of Massachusetts, made no bones about liking beef stroganoff better than clam chowder.

LYNDON JOHNSON was about as colorful in his food choices as in everything else... he ate tapioca pudding every day for lunch. And his favorite drink was the ill-fated Fresca.

RICHARD NIXON was known for his lunch: cottage cheese and ketchup.

RONALD REAGAN, considered ketchup a vegetable, never met a jelly bean he didn't like, and loved macaroni and cheese so much that he had it served on Air Force One... whenever first lady Nancy was not on board.

THE PENNY

Suppose our civilization were destroyed and our cities laid completely in waste. Suppose in twenty-thousand years an archaeologist from another society were poking around the ruins of your city. If he could dig up just one penny, he would know this about us:

> The coin is made of a blend of metals, that would tell him we were miners and knew the science of metalurgy.

> By the shape of the coin, a perfect circle, he'd know that we understood geometry.

> The date on the face of the coin would show him we understood arithmetic and that we had a calendar.

> The portrait of Abraham Lincoln would mark us as artists who had an advanced culture.

> The words "United States" would let him know that we were a federated group of local communities bound together by a strong central government.

> The phrase "e pluribus unum" would tell him we were scholars who knew foreign languages.

> The word "liberty" right on the face of the penny would let the archaeologist know that our country sought to guarantee freedom for every man.

> And finally that phrase "In God We Trust". It would tell him we had a moral law. It would let him know that we had grown strong and mighty under God's great hand.

And then, considering the penny, he would wonder... why did they ever go astray?

FIRSTS

1854   Baby Show... Springfield, OH

1869   Jukebox... San Francisco

1878   Telephone Directory in the world was published in New Haven, Connecticut. It was a single sheet of paper listing 50 customers.

1884   Toothbrush factory... Florence, MA

1889   Pay telephone booth in the world

1897   Comic strip in the world appeared in the New York Journal

1899   Juvenile Court... Chicago

1913   Gasoline service station opened in Pittsburgh, Pennsylvania

1921   Bathing Beauty Contest ... Atlantic City

1925   Motel... San Luis Obispo, CA

1933   Comic book in the world printed in Waterbury, Connecticut

1933   Drive-in movie theater ... Camden, NJ

1934   Laundromat... Fort Worth, TX

AMERICAN INVENTIONS

Ball point pens
Barbed wire
Baseball
Basketball
Calliope
Cash register
Cellophane
Coca Cola
Coffee percolator (James Nason / Franklin MASS 1853)
Condensed milk
Crossword puzzles
Escalator (Gimbel Bros. Department Store/Philadelphia 1901)
Eskimo Pie
Ferris Wheel (George Washington Gale Ferris)
Graham crackers
Hearing aid (Miller Reese Hutchinson)
Hot dogs
Ice cream cones
Ice Cream Sodas (O. P. Bauer owned a confectionery store in Denver, Colorado. One hot summer day in 1871 he experimented with some ice cream and carbonated water and created the first ice cream soda.)
Lightning rods
Outboard motors for boats
Parking meters
Popsicle
Potato chips
Railroad sleeping cars
Rocking chair (Benjamin Franklin)
Safety Pin (Walter Hunt)
Shredded wheat and corn flakes
Swivel chair (Thomas Jefferson)
Toothpaste tube
Vaseline
Zipper (Whitcomb Judson 1893)
... and Mickey Mouse!

SECTION SEVEN

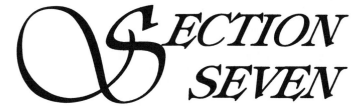

Politics

WELFARE WARFARE

**Actual letters received by the Welfare Department
Orange County, Florida**

I am forwarding my marriage certificate and my six children. I have seven but one died which was baptized on a half sheet of paper.

I am writing to say that my baby was born two years old. When do I get my money.

I cannot get sick pay. I have six children, can you tell me why?

I am glad to report that my husband who was reported missing is now dead.

This is my eighth child. What are you going to do about it?

Please find out for certain if my husband is dead. The man I live with now can't eat or do nothing till he knows.

I am very annoyed to find that you have branded my boy as illiterate as this is a dirty lie. I was married to his father a week before he was born.

I am forwarding my marriage certificate and my three children, one of which was a mistake as you will see.

In answer to your letter, I have given birth to a boy weighing 101 lbs. I hope this is satisfactory.

My husband got his project cut off two weeks ago and I haven't had any relief since. Unless I get my husband's money pretty soon, I will be forced to lead an immortal life.

You have changed my little boy to a girl. Will this make any difference?

Please send money at once as I have fallen in error with my landlord.

In accordance with instructions I have given birth to twins in the enclosed envelope.

I want money quick as I can get it. I have been in bed with the doctor for two weeks and he doesn't do me no good. If things don't improve, I will have to send for another doctor.

CRIME TIME

All of these are (or once were) real laws.

It is a crime . . .

. . . to bathe less than once a year in Kentucky, and more than once a week in Boston.

. . . to catch mice in Cleveland without a hunting license.

. . . to tie a giraffe to a telephone pole in Atlanta.

. . . to whistle underwater in Vermont.

. . . to put a skunk in your boss's desk in Michigan.

. . . to own a copy of THE ENCYCLOPEDIA BRITANNICA in Texas, because it contains a liquor recipe.

. . . to get a fish drunk anywhere in the state of Oklahoma.

. . . to go to church in Georgia without a loaded rifle.

. . . to give your sweetheart in Idaho a box of candy weighing less than 50 pounds.

. . . to eat a snake on Sunday anywhere in Kansas.

. . . to eat in a place that is on fire in Chicago.

. . . to go to bed with your boots on in North Dakota.

. . . to ride in a baby carriage in Roderfield, West Virginia, unless you are a baby.

INCOMPETENCE IN LAW

In Seattle it is illegal to carry a concealed weapon that is more than 6 feet long.

In Danville, Pennsylvania, fire hydrants must be checked one hour before all fires.

In Lakefield, Ontario, the City council passed noise-abatement legislation permitting birds to sing for 30 minutes during the day and 15 minutes at night.

A San Francisco ordinance bans the reuse of confetti.

The Treasury Department's form F4473, devised to record gun sales, inquires of the purchaser: "Are you a fugitive from justice?"

When Dr. John Ziegler of Cincinnati wrote to Washington for a federal publication called HANDBOOK FOR EMERGENCIES, he carefully identified it by its code number #15700. Two weeks later 15,700 copies arrived at his house.

The Department of Agriculture spent $133,417 on a study from which it learned that mothers prefer children's clothing that does not require ironing.

In Pittsburgh, Pennsylvania, the Governor was on hand to open the new $60,000,000 Post Office. After the ribbon cutting ceremony, he walked into the lobby to post the first letter. Five minutes later, after wandering through the facility, it was discovered that the architect had forgotten to install even one mail drop.

It's illegal to give alcoholic beverages to a moose in Fairbanks, Alaska.

In North Carolina, farmers cannot use elephants to plow their fields.

Barbers in Waterloo, Nebraska, are banned from eating onions between the hours of 7 a.m and 7 p.m.

Clergymen are barred from telling jokes from the pulpit in Nicholas County, West Virginia.

Sinners in Fredericksburg, Virginia, may not sit on their front porch and read the Sunday paper during Church services.

In Los Angeles, ladies are banned from hanging their lingerie outside during the winter.

INCOMPENTANCE IN LAW...Continued

It's against the law to fall asleep in the bathtub in Detroit.

An ordinance in Pittsburgh, forbids housewives from hiding dust under a rug or carpet.

Snoopy wives are in trouble in Montana, where it's a felony for a woman to open and read her husband's mail.

No South Dakota female over 50 years of age may leave her house to strike up a conversation with a married man over 20.

The town of Burns, Oregon, says it's O.K. for horse owners to bring their steeds into local taverns and nightclubs... but only if they've paid an admission fee for the animal first.

A motorist traveling along a country road in Pennsylvania after dark must stop each mile and send up a rocket signal... then wait 10 minutes for the road to be cleared of livestock before proceeding.

The law in Shaftsbury, Vermont bans all local citizens from "driving ugly automobiles." Anyone found guilty will be fined a minimum of $5.00 and serve up to three days in jail.

The New Hampshire Legislature passed this traffic stopper: Any vehicles meeting an intersection must stop. Each must wait for the other to pass. Neither can proceed until the other is gone.

In Memphis, Tennessee, frogs are prohibited from croaking after 11 pm. No mention is made of who will explain this to the frogs.

It is illegal in Fayetteville, Tennessee, for a girl to do cartwheels while crossing a street.

No man, woman, or child in Nacogdoches, Texas, is allowed to crack pecan shells while sitting in a church service.

Don't sit on your boyfriends lap in Lawton, Oklahoma, just because he asks you to. The law states, "No young woman shall sit on a man's lap without a cushion or a pillow under her."

In Willow springs, Missouri, it's illegal for a man to stroll around town while carrying his shoes in his pockets.

In Birmingham, Alabama, all streetcar lines are prohibited from using flat wheels on their cars.

❧ Politically Correct ❧

Don't call that schlub a "fatty" for it's simply not allowed;
   He's now **physically expansive** or **nutritionally endowed**.
That child repeating seventh grade... he's not a knucklehead,
   Sophisticatedly persistent is the phrase to use instead.

Don't talk of dwarfs or midgets, both are terms to be revised,
   Today they're known as person of **non-excessive size**.
You'll find you're not offending any group or race or sect,
   As long as what you're saying is politically correct.

Our nation has no Indians, in case you haven't heard,
   Indigenous Americans is now the term preferred.
Don't call that drifter homeless, that's the no-no of the year;
   He's a **worker in transition** or an **urban pioneer**.

Don't call that guy in women's clothes a weirdo or a freak;
   He's a **fashion non-comformist** with a life-style that's unique.
No lack of sensitivity will anyone detect,
   As long as every comment is politically correct.

To psychopathic killers, nicer labels we're now giving;
   They're **gentlemen who specialize** in terminating living.
Don't call that creep a rapist, he might think you were unkind;
   He's a **sexual crusader who's assertively inclined**.

As for those scuzzy pushers, hooking kids throughout the land,
   They're **inner city merchants with a product in demand**.
So make certain that you're careful of the words that you select,
   And we guarantee you'll always be Politically Correct.

COWS AND CAPITALISM

SOCIALISM:
> You have two cows and give one to your neighbor.

COMMUNISM:
> You have two cows.
> The government takes both and gives you the milk.

FASCISM:
> You have two cows.
> The government takes both of them and sells you the milk.

NAZISM:
> You have two cows.
> The government takes both of them and shoots you.

NEW DEALISM:
> You have two cows. The government takes both:
> shoots one, milks the other, and throws the milk away.

CAPITALISM:
> You have two cows. You sell one and buy a bull.

Section
Eight

RANDOM
Information

I DIDN'T KNOW THAT EITHER

A few years ago I wrote a book called I DIDN'T KNOW THAT. These are a few items that got missed in the first edition.

A TEASPOON A DAY . . .

Ketchup once was sold as a patent medicine. In the 1830's it enjoyed a measure of popularity in the United States as DR. MILES COMPOUND EXTRACT OF TOMATO, guaranteed to relieve a multitude of ills.

ON THE ROAD.

There are half a million more cars in Los Angeles than there are people.

FAVORITE SON.

No U. S. President was an only child.

GOOD TO THE LAST BEAN.

The annual harvest of an entire coffee tree is required for a single pound of ground coffee. Every tree bears up to six pounds of beans, which are reduced to a pound after the beans are roasted and ground.

NAME THAT TUNE.

When it was first published in September of 1814 in the Baltimore Patriot, it was called "The Defense of Fort McHenry." A month later the title was changed to "The Star Spangled Banner."

TWO FORKS FOR A QUARTER.

Martha Washington's table service dinnerware was the source of the silver that went into the first U. S. coins.

FEAR FOR FUN.

For amusement it was agreed by four friends holidaying in Switzerland that each would write a ghost story. Percy B. Shelly, George Byron, and Dr. John William Polidori never finished theirs. Only 18-year-old Mary Wollstonecraft did. She published it anonymously two years later, with a preface by her husband, Shelley. And Mary Shelley's novel about Dr. Victor Frankenstein and his monstrous creation has become a classic.

HORATIO ALGER CARNEGIE.

At the age of 12, Andrew Carnegie worked as a millhand for $1.20 a week. He eventually bought the mill and half a century later sold his steel company for half a billion dollars.

{I DIDN'T KNOW THAT EITHER}

WOMAN OF THE YEAR(S).
The woman who has appeared most often on the cover of Time magazine is the Virgin Mary . . . 10 times.

WATCH IT.
Having survived a barrel ride over Niagara Falls in 1911 that broke "nearly every bone" in his body, Bobby Leech stepped on a banana peel and died of complications from the fall.

MOMMY, MOMMY, MOMMY, MOMMY, MOMMY, MOMMY.
The average married woman in the 17th century America gave birth to 13 children.

STORM WARNING.
Lightning kills more people in the United States than any other natural disaster... an average of 400 dead and 1,000 injured every year.

COOL IT.
Eskimos use refrigerators to keep food FROM freezing.

ET TU DRIVER?
Julius Caesar was compelled by increasing traffic congestion to ban all wheeled vehicles in Rome during the hours of daylight.

HANDLE WITH CARE.
Benjamin Franklin was cautious in performing his famous kite experiment in which he charged a Leyden jar with electricity drawn from the clouds. The first two men who tried to repeat the experiment were electrocuted.

WELL BLOW ME DOWN.
The windiest city in the U.S. is not Chicago... it's Fargo, North Dakota, where winds average 14.4 MPH. Winds in Chicago average only 10.6 MPH.

{I DIDN'T KNOW THAT EITHER}

ENCORE, ENCORE.
Every time Johnny Carson was introduced with the TONIGHT SHOW theme music, Paul Anka got another $200.00. He composed the song in 1962. That's over a million and a half dollars!

HAPPY LEFTOVERS.
When oil was discovered in 1859 it was used primarily for kerosene, naphtha and petroleum jelly. One by-product, gasoline, was discarded as a nuisance. There was no practical use for it until years later, when the automobile was invented.

WHAT'S YOUR HURRY?
Changing lanes won't get you to your destination much quicker, according to a Los Angeles police study. Four cars traveled 10 miles in traffic on the Hollywood freeway. One was allowed to dart back and forth between lanes. The others couldn't. The result? The speed demon finished only 82 seconds ahead of the slowest vehicle.

NO WONDER A DAY AT THE BEACH IS SO TIRING.
Sunlight puts weight on the earth's surface . . . two pounds per square mile.

NOW . . . WHERE'S THE PALM TREE?
The liquid inside young coconuts can be used as a substitute for blood plasma in a emergency.

BUT WHAT ABOUT THE THOMPSON SEEDLESS?
The purple dye used in the U.S. to stamp meat is made from grape skins.

I KNEW THAT!
The most common surnames in North America are, in order: Smith, Johnson, Williams, Brown and Jones.

BAD NEWS TRAVELS FAST.
Garlic rubbed on the soles of your feet will be noticeable on your breath in one hour.

—— How Long Did It Take? ——

The Wright Brothers' first flight was over in just 12 seconds.

The Boston Tea Party lasted less than 3 hours.

Columbus' first trip to the New World required 2 months and 9 days.

In 1876 Battle of the little Bighorn when General George Custer and his 264 men were wiped out by 4,000 Indians lasted about 30 minutes.

But the gunfight at O.K. Corral, pitting Wyatt Earp and three comrades against four rivals, took just 30 seconds.

The attack on Fort Sumter in South Carolina, which began the Civil War, lasted 34 hours before the union garrison surrendered.

The first tremor of the 1906 San Francisco earthquake began at 5:13 A.M. on April 18. The quake ended 1 minute and 14 seconds later . . . but the fires that resulted lasted 3 1/2 days.

Two hours and 40 minutes elapsed between the time the Titanic struck an iceberg in the north Atlantic and the moment it slipped beneath the waves.

Charles Lindbergh took 33 hours, 29 minutes and 30 seconds to become the first man to fly solo across the Atlantic.

The explosion and burning of the dirigible Hindenburg took 2 minutes and 20 seconds.

The attack on Pearl harbor, which cost the United States an incredible 16 ships and more than 2400 lives, lasted for about two hours.

The atomic bomb that destroyed Hiroshima took 43 seconds to fall from an American bomber to its detonation point 1980 feet above its target . . . and then just a split second to obliterate the center of the city.

Neil Armstrong, the first man to walk on the moon, began his historic stroll at 10:56 P.M. on July 20, 1969, and returned to his spacecraft 2 hours and 21 minutes later.

For the Congress to spend one billion dollars it takes 10 hours and 20 minutes.

A SAMPLING OF PHOBIAS

Ablutophobia...	Fear of washing or bathing
Acousticophobia...	Fear of noise
Acrophobia...	Fear of high places
Agiraphobia...	Fear of open or public places
Aichmophobia...	Fear of sharp instruments
Arachnophobia...	Fear of spiders
Ailurophobia...	Fear of cats
Batrachophobia...	Fear of frogs
Chromatophobia...	Fear of certain colors
Chronophobia...	Fear of time
Claustrophobia...	Fear of confined spaces
Climacophobia...	Fear of stairs
Cynophobia...	Fear of dogs
Ergophobia...	Fear of work
Erythrophobia...	Fear of blushing
Hydrophobia..	Fear of water
Kenophobia...	Fear of empty spaces
Keraunophobia...	Fear of lightning and thunder
Lachanophobia...	Fear of vegetables
Microphobia...	Fear of germs
Mysophobia...	Fear of dirt
Ophidophobia...	Fear of snakes
Nyctophobia...	Fear of the dark
Pediophobia...	Fear of dolls
Phobophobia...	Fear of fear
Photophobia...	Fear of light
Pluviophobia...	Fear of rain
Staurophobia...	Fear of crucifixes
Triskaidekaphobia...	Fear of the number 13
Zoophobia...	Fear of animals

Source: The Encyclopedia of Phobias,
Fears, and Anxieties 1989

And here are a few other phobias to consider:

Ouchophobia	Fear of pain
Gotchaphobia	Fear of guilt
Foolaphobia	Fear of knowledge
Noaphobia	Fear of progress

Source: The Derric Johnson Encyclopedia
of Phobias and Pain 1993

═══TOP 14 FEARS═══

(According to a survey of 3,000 U.S. residents)

1. Speaking before a group (41%)

2. Heights   (32%)

3. Insects and bugs   (22%)

3. Financial problems   (22%)

3. Deep water   (22%)

6. Sickness   (19%)

6. Death   (19%)

6. Flying   (19%)

9. Loneliness   (14%)

10. Dogs   (11%)

11. Driving/riding in a car   (9%)

12. Darkness   (8%)

12. Elevators   (8%)

14. Escalators   (5%)

Section
Nine

Relationships

• • • • THE RULES • • • •

1. The female always makes The Rules.

2. The Rules are subject to change at any time without prior notification.

3. No male can possibly know all The Rules.

4. If the female suspects the male knows all The Rules, she must immediately change some or all of The Rules.

5. The female is never wrong.

6. If the female is wrong, it is because of a flagrant misunderstanding, which was a direct result of something the male did or said wrong.

7. If The Rule #6 applies, the male must apologize immediately for causing the misunderstanding.

8. The female can change her mind at any given point in time.

9. The male must never change his mind without express written consent from the female.

10. The female has every right to be angry or upset at any time.

11. The male must remain calm at all times, unless the female wants him to be angry or upset.

13. Any attempt to document these Rules could result in bodily harm.

14. If the female has PMS all Rules are null and void!

How Men Really Behave

Q. What's a man's idea of helping with the housework?
A. Lifting his legs so you can vacuum.

Q. What's the difference between a man and E.T.?
A. E.T. called home.

Q. Why is psychoanalysis a lot quicker for men than women?
A. When it's time to go back to his childhood, he's already there.

Q. Why is it good that there are female astronauts?
A. When the crew gets lost in space, at least the women will ask for directions.

Q. How do men define a 50-50 relationship?
A. They cook/we eat; they iron/we wrinkle; they clean/we dirty.

Q. What's the best way to force a man to do sit-ups?
A. Put the remote control between his toes.

Q. How do men exercise at the beach?
A. By sucking in the tummies every time they see a bikini.

Q. If one woman can wash one stack of dishes in one hour, how many stacks of dishes can four men wash in four hours?
A. None. They'll set down and watch football on television.

Q. What does a man consider a seven-course meal?
A. A hot dog and a six-pack.

Q. How are men like noodles?
A. They're always in hot water, they lack taste and they need dough.

How Can You Be Perfectly Miserable?

Begin by telling yourself that no one understands you. Nobody can judge an Indian until he has walked in his moccasins.

Then figure that what is wrong for others is all right for you because you are different.

If you do not believe this, turn the coin over and say, "Well, if I am wrong, at least I have plenty of company."

Then, too, you should convince yourself that no one loves you and they will be sorry some day for their indifference.

Keep telling yourself that you have as much right to happiness as anyone else and write the ticket your own way. After all, if you don't take good care of your own self, who will?

By all means, feel sorry for yourself and be thoroughly convinced that you are the only one in the world who has suffered the things you have.

When because of this people begin to avoid you, tell yourself it is their fault and that as Christians they should be more considerate.

Find someone else you can find fault with. This way you won't have to face reality with yourself.

Forget the Bible as a guide for life. It may make you miserable and God expects you to be happy.

When the sky falls and life grown meaningless, simply ask yourself how God can be so mean?

❧ A Friend Is... ☙

A friend is someone who makes you feel totally acceptable.

❧☙

A friend is someone who asks how you are...
and waits for the answer.

❧☙

A friend is someone who knows all about you...
and loves you anyway.

❧☙

A friend is someone who walks in...
when everyone else walks out.

❧☙

A friend hears the song in your heart...
and sings it to you when your memory fails.

❧☙

Love is a flower... but friendship is a tree.

THINGS COULD GET WORSE

You remember the old saw... "Things were really going bad, and a friend of mine said, 'Cheer up! Things could get worse.' So I cheered up... and sure enough... things got worse!"

PORTLAND, OREGON... A Shopkeeper advertised for a night watchman. The next night he was robbed.

BIRMINGHAM, ALABAMA... A woman fought hard in court for a large alimony settlement and was awarded a thousand dollars a month. Her ex-husband has every payment delivered in nickels... 420 pounds of them every month... UNWRAPPED!

PITTSBURGH, PENNSYLVANIA... A cheating husband was found out by his wife. She became so depressed that she jumped off the balcony of their high-rise apartment. By sheer coincidence, her husband walked right underneath her... and she crashed down on top of him. Thanks to the husband breaking her fall, the woman lived... but he died.

IRVINE, CALIFORNIA... And then there was the jealous wife who persuaded herself that her husband was having an affair with a friend she knew who drove a flashy sports car. When the wife spotted the car parked outside her husband's office building, she used a knife to slash the car's seats to ribbons and wreck its paint job. When she stormed into her husband's office to catch him with the "other woman", she found him alone. After she told him what she had done, her face went white with horror as he explained: "I knew you always liked that car, so I got you one just like it as a surprise birthday present. That's your car!"

BATON ROUGE, LOUISIANA... Seeing a cockroach in the bathroom, an insect-fearing woman sprayed the room with Raid. Then she dumped the dead cockroach down the toilet and sprayed even more Raid after it. Minutes later, her husband used the bathroom, sat on the toilet and when he lit a cigarette, the Raid fumes exploded, severely burning his backside. As the ambulance crew carried the husband from the house, the woman told them how his injury happened. The crew laughed so hard, they dropped the stretcher and the husband broke his leg.

BOISE, IDAHO... A carpet layer finished tacking down the last edge when he noticed his pack of cigarettes was missing and then spotted a lump near the middle of the rug. Rather than undo his work, he hammered the mound flat and went to his truck where he found his cigarettes on the dashboard. Confused, he went back into the house where the homeowner asked him, "Have you seen my parakeet? He got out of his cage and I can't find him."

NO SWEAT

Who needs a physical fitness program? Most of us get enough
exercise . . . . . . jumping to conclusions
flying off the handle
dodging responsibilities
bending rules

running down everything
circulating rumors
passing the buck
stirring up trouble

sawing logs
shooting the bull
polishing the apple
digging up excuses

slinging mud
throwing our weight around
beating the system
and pushing our luck.

GIRL-TALK

From some notable... and quotable women.

Husbands are like fires. They go out if left unattended.

Zsa Zsa Gabor

If you obey all the rules... you miss all the fun.

Katherine Hepburn

It goes without saying that you should never have more children than you have car windows.

Erma Bombeck

I suppose when they reach a certain age some men are afraid to grow up. It seems the older the men get, the younger their new wives become.

Elizabeth Taylor

My idea of superwoman is someone who scrubs her own floors.

Bette Midler

Some of us are becoming the men we wanted to marry.

Gloria Steinem

Motherhood is tough. If you just want a wonderful little creature to love, you can get a puppy.

Barbara Walters

A man has to be a Senator Joe McCarthy to be called ruthless. All a woman has to do is put you on hold.

Marlo Thomas

Mistakes are part of the dues one pays for a full life.

Sophia Loren

Love is a game that two can play and both win.

Eva Gabor

Success for me is having 10 honeydew melons and eating only the top half of each one.

Barbara Streisand

A child of 1 can be taught not to do certain dangerous things... such as touch a hot stove, turn on the gas, pull lamps off their tables by their cords, or wake Mommy before noon.

Joan Rivers

If truth is beauty, how come no one has their hair done in the library?

Lily Tomlin

The Snake That Poisons Everybody

It topples governments,
  wrecks marriages,
  ruins careers,
  busts reputations,
  causes heartaches,
    nightmares,
    indigestion,
  spawns suspicion,
  generates grief,
  dispatches innocent people to cry in their pillows.

Even its name hisses.
            It's called gossip.
            Office gossip.
            Shop gossip.
            Party gossip.

        It makes headlines and headaches.

        Before you repeat a story, ask yourself:
                            Is it true?
                            Is it fair?
                        Is it necessary?

                    If not, shut up!

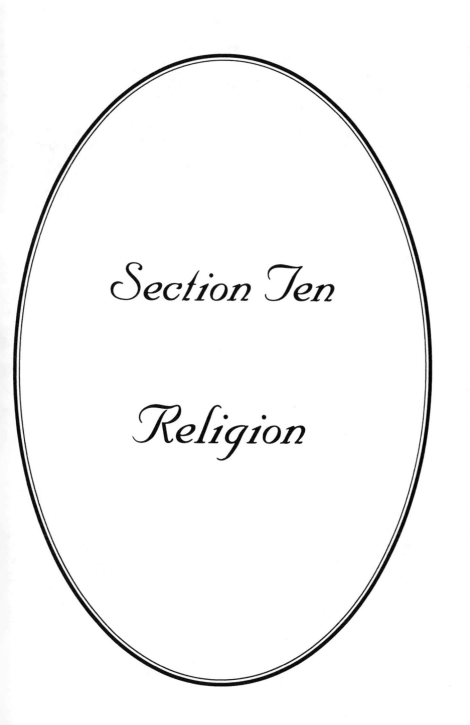

Section Ten

Religion

B•U•L•L•E•T•I•N • B•L•O•O•P•E•R•S

Actual Messages Taken from Church Newsletters

This afternoon there will be a meeting in the South and North ends of the Church. People will be baptized at both ends.

Next Sunday is Easter and Mrs. Anderson will come forward and lay an egg on the altar.

On Sunday, a special collection will be taken to help defray the expense of the new carpet. All those wishing to do something on the carpet, come forward and get a piece of paper.

A bean supper will be held Saturday evening in the Church basement. Music will follow.

The Church Choir will begin practice for the Christmas Cantata next Wednesday at 7:00 p.m. We have a special need for men's voices, but all parts are welcome.

Tonight's sermon: <u>WHAT IS HELL?</u> Come early and listen to our choir practicing.

The outreach committee has enlisted 25 visitors to make calls on people who are not afflicted with any church.

The Ladies Bible Study will be held Thursday morning at 10. All the ladies are invited to lunch in the Fellowship Hall after the B.S. is done.

The sermon this morning: **<u>JESUS WALKS ON THE WATER</u>**
The sermon tonight: **<u>SEARCHING FOR JESUS</u>**

The rosebud on the altar this morning is to announce the birth of David Allen, the sin of Mr. and Mrs. Julius Belser.

THE BUILDING IS ON FIRE

During a recent ecumenical gathering, someone rushed in shouting, "The building is on fire!"

..... The Methodists gathered in a corner and prayed.

..... The Baptists yelled, "Where is the water?"

The Quakers quietly praised God for the blessing that fire brings

..... The Lutherans posted a notice on the door declaring the fire was evil.

..... The Catholics took pledges to cover the damage.

..... The Pentecostals praised God and shouted, "Holy Smoke!"

..... The Fundamentalists proclaimed, "It's the vengeance of God."

..... The Christian Scientists agreed among themselves that there really was no fire at all.

..... The Presbyterians appointed a chair-person who was to appoint a committee to look into the matter and make a written report to the Session.

..... The Salvation Army took their drums and brass, formed a parade and marched out of the building.

THE *NO-EXCUSE* SUNDAY

In order to make it possible for everyone to attend church next week, we are planning a special no-excuse Sunday.

1. Cots will be placed in the vestibule for those who say, "Sunday is my only day for sleeping in."

2. Eye drops will be available for those whose eyes are tired from watching TV too late on Saturday night.

3. We will have steel helmets for those who believe the roof will cave in if they show up for church services.

4. Blankets will be furnished for those who complain that the church is too cold. Fans will be on hand for those who say the church is too hot.

5. We will have hearing aids for the parishioners who say, "The pastor doesn't talk loudly enough." There will be cotton for those who say, "The pastor talks too loudly."

6. Score cards will be available for those who wish to count the hypocrites.

7. We guarantee that some relatives will be present for those who like to go visiting on Sunday.

8. There will be TV dinners available for those who claim they can't go to church and cook dinner, too.

9. One section of the church will have some trees and grass for those who see God in nature, especially on the golf course.

10. The sanctuary will be decorated with both Christmas poinsettias and Easter lilies to create a familiar environment for those who have never seen the church without them.

WHY I DO NOT ATTEND THE MOVIES

1. The manager of the theater never called on me.

2. I did go a few times, but no one spoke to me. People who go there aren't very friendly.

3. Every time I go they ask me for money.

4. Not all people in the films live up to the same standards as mine.

5. I went so much as a child, I've decided that I've had all the entertainment I need.

6. The performance lasts too long. I can't set still for an hour and half.

7. I don't care for some of the people I see and meet at the theater.

8. I don't always agree with what I see and hear.

9. The music in the movies is not always what I like.

10. Most of the shows are held in the evenings, and that's the only time I have to be at home with my family.

How to be a good kid in church.

1. **IT'S NOT NICE TO SPEAK WHEN THERE IS SINGING OR PRAYING.**
   Wait till there is silence, then talk LOUDLY so you can be heard.

2. **NEVER FALL ASLEEP IN CHURCH.**
   Stay awake by squirming and wiggling a lot.

3. **HONOR THY FATHER.**
   Tell everybody how much he put in the collection plate.

4. **YOU ARE IN GOD'S HOUSE.**
   Ask to see His bathroom.

5. **GOODNESS IS ALWAYS REWARDED.**
   Tell your mom you're being good and want the candy that's in her purse.

6. **UNDERSTAND THY NEIGHBOR.**
   Stare at the people behind you and try to get them to make faces at you.

7. **LEARN ALL YOU CAN ABOUT RELIGION.**
   Ask why the seats are called "pews".

SURVEY OF CHURCH MEMBERS

5%   of reported church members do not exist.

10%   cannot be found.

20%   never pray.

30%   never attend church.

40%   never give to any cause.

50%   never go to Sunday School.

60%   never go to church on Sunday night.

70%   never give to missions.

75%   never read the Bible personally.

80%   never go to any prayer meeting.

90%   never have family worship.

95%   never have been influential in winning a soul to Christ.

TAKE A LOOK IN THE BOOK

"I will delight myself in Thy statutes" Psalm 119:16

That seems almost too simple, doesn't it"
Almost naive.
At best, it sounds old fashioned and quaint.

I mean, who comes to the Word of God with delight anymore?
Aren't we more sophisticated than that today?

We come with determination
diligence
discipline and
a sense of duty.

We bring charts
commentaries
concordances
dictionaries
encyclopedias
guides
graphs
maps
outlines
summaries
systems and
study helps.

We search for applications
attitudes
comparisons
concepts
contrasts
commands
cross-references
examples
exhortations
illustrations
repetitions
statistics and
warnings.

TAKE A LOOK IN THE BOOK... Continued

We discover key words
key verses
key thoughts
key statements and
key chapters.
We develop word studies
topic studies
character studies
and prayer studies.

We use translations
paraphrases
editions
versions
and revisions of versions.

We read and
re-read
until we become well versed.

We are experts on Bible Study Methods.

What could the Psalmist have been thinking of:
"I will delight myself in Thy statutes..."
Surely, this approach is too childish
for mature Bible Students.

Still...
... some of us wonder...

... do you suppose it would be all right with the
Father if we were to sort of ditch school once in a while and just curl up with
a good book?

It really seems delightful.

What Great Leaders Have Said About The Bible

GEORGE WASHINGTON   It is impossible to rightly govern the world without the Bible.

JOHN ADAMS   The Bible is the best book in the world. It contains more than all the libraries I have seen.

THOMAS JEFFERSON   The Bible makes the best people in the world.

JOHN QUINCY ADAMS   It is an invaluable and inexhaustible mine of knowledge and virtue.

ANDREW JACKSON   That Book, sir, is the rock on which our Republic rests.

ZACHARY TAYLOR   It was for the love of the truths of this great book that our fathers abandoned their native shore for the wilderness.

ABRAHAM LINCOLN   But for this Book we could not know right from wrong. I believe the Bible is the best gift God has ever given to man.

ULYSSES S. GRANT   The Bible is the Anchor of our liberties.

RUTHERFORD B. HAYES   The best religion the world has ever known is the religion of the Bible. It builds up all that is good.

BENJAMIN HARRISON   It is out of the Word of God that a system has come to make life sweet.

What Great Leaders Have Said... Continued

WILLIAM McKINLEY

The more profoundly we study this wonderful Book... the better citizens we will become.

THEODORE ROOSEVELT

No educated man can afford to be ignorant of the Bible.

WOODROW WILSON

The Bible is the one supreme source of the revelation of the meaning of life.

HERBERT HOOVER

The whole of the inspirations of our civilization springs from the teachings of Christ. To read the Bible is a necessity of American life.

FRANKLIN D. ROOSEVELT

It is a fountain of strength. I feel that a comprehensive study of the Bible is a liberal education for anyone.

DWIGHT D. EISENHOWER

In the highest sense the Bible is to us the unique repository of eternal spiritual truths.

RONALD REAGAN

No book has so molded the life of a nation as the Bible has shaped America. It has been America's hope, its foundation, its molder of character. The Bible has sustained America throughout its 200-year history and is our only hope of security for the years ahead.

JESUS CHRIST

It is written, man shall not live by bread alone, but by every word that proceedeth out of the mouth of God.

HOW **BIG** IS GOD?

Let the thickness of this page represent the distance of Earth to Sun (93,000,000 miles . . . 8 light minutes).

✳ ✳ ✳

Then the distance to the nearest star is a 71 foot-high stack of paper (4 1/3 light years).

✳ ✳ ✳

And the diameter of our own galaxy is a 310 mile-high stack of paper (100,000 light years).

✳ ✳ ✳

While the edge of our known universe is not reached until the pile of paper is 31,000,000 miles high (1/3 of the way to the sun).

✳ ✳ ✳

Galaxies are as common as blades of grass in the meadow. They number perhaps 100 billion.

✳ ✳ ✳

Palomar estimates that 1,000,000 galaxies can be seen inside the bowl of the Big Dipper alone.

Section
Eleven

Seasonal

RESOLUTIONS FOR A BETTER NEW YEAR

Vow to do some of the things you've always wanted to do but couldn't find the time.

Call up a forgotten friend.

Drop an old grudge and replace it with some pleasant memories.

Share a funny story with someone whose spirits are dragging. A good laugh can be very good medicine.

Vow not to make a promise you don't think you can keep.

Give a soft answer.

Free yourself of envy and malice. Encourage some youth to do his or her best. Share your experience and offer support. Young people need role models.

Make a genuine effort to stay in closer touch with family and good friends.

Resolve to stop magnifying small problems and shooting from the lip. Words that you have to eat can be hard to digest.

Find the time to be kind and thoughtful. All of us have the same allotment... 24 hours a day.

Give a compliment. It might give someone a badly needed lift.

Think things through.

Be kind.

Apologize when you realize you are wrong. An apology never diminishes a person. It elevates him.

Don't blow your own horn. If you've done something praiseworthy, someone will notice eventually.

Try to understand a point of view that is different from your own. Few things are 100% one way or another.

Examine the demands you make on others.

Lighten up. When you feel like blowing your top, ask yourself, "Will it matter a week from today?"

Laugh the loudest when the joke is on you.

The sure way to have a friend is to be one. We are all connected by our humanity, and we need each other.

Avoid malcontents and pessimists. They drag you down and contribute nothing.

Don't discourage a beginner from trying something risky.

Be optimistic. The can do spirit is the fuel that makes things go

Go to war against animosity and complacency.

Give credit when it's due... and even when it isn't. It will make you look good.

Read something uplifting. Deep-six the trash. You shouldn't eat garbage... why put it in your head?

Don't abandon your old-fashioned principles. They never go out of style.

When courage is needed, ask yourself, "If not me... who? If not now... when?"

Take better care of yourself. Remember, you're all you've got.

Return those books you borrowed.

Take those photos out of the drawer and put them in an album.

If you see litter on the sidewalk, pick it up instead of walking over it.

Give yourself a reality check. Phoniness is transparent and it is tiresome.

Take pleasure in the beauty and the wonders of nature. A flower is still a miracle.

Walk tall and smile more.

Don't be afraid to say, "I love you." They are the best words in the world.

During This New Year May You Have....

...enough happiness to keep you sweet.

...enough distress to keep you strong.

...enough sorrow to keep you human.

...enough hope to keep you happy.

...enough determination to make today better than yesterday.

...enough failure to keep you humble.

...enough success to keep you eager.

...enough friends to give you comfort.

...enough wealth to meet your needs.

...enough enthusiasm to take you to tomorrow.

Jesus and Alexander The Great

Jesus and Alexander died at 33!

One lived and died for himself. One lived and died for others.
The Greek died on a throne . . . the Jew died on a cross.
One's life a triumph seemed . . . the other but a loss.
One led vast armies forth . . . the other walked alone.
One shed a whole world's blood . . . the other gave his own.
One conquered the world in life and lost it all in death.
The other conquered death in life
    and won the world through faith

Jesus and Alexander died at 33!

One died in Babylon . . . the other at Calvary.
One gained all for himself . . . the other, himself he gave.
One conquered every tongue . . . the other every grave.
One made himself God . . . the other made himself less.
One lived to torment . . . the other but to bless.
When died the Greek, forever fell his throne of swords.
But Jesus died to live forever,
King of Kings and Lord of Lords.

Jesus and Alexander died at 33!

The Greek made all men slaves . . . the Jew made all men free.
One built a throne on war . . . the other built on love.
One was born on earth . . . the other from above.
One was a baby who became a king.
The other a king who became a baby.
The Greek forever died . . . The Jew forever lives!

    Alexander died at 33! But at 33... Jesus lived again!

    And He proved that if we believed in Him... we could, too!

IT'S FRIDAY...
But Sunday's Coming

It's Friday   Jesus was nailed dead on a cross.

                                          . . . but Sunday's coming.

It's Friday   Mary's crying her eyes out 'cause her baby Jesus is dead.

                                          . . . but Sunday's coming.

It's Friday   The disciples are running in every direction like sheep without a shepherd.

                                          . . . but Sunday's coming.

It's Friday   Pilate is strutting around, washing his hands 'cause he thinks he's got all the power and the victory.

                                          . . . but Sunday's coming.

It's Friday   People are saying, "As things have been, so shall they always be. You can't change anything in this life."

                                          . . . but Sunday's coming.

It's Friday   Satan's doing a little jig saying, "I control the world."

                                          . . . but Sunday's coming.

It's Friday   The temple veil is ripped from top to bottom.
The earth shakes. The rocks split and the tombs open.
The centurion screamed in fear, "Truly he was the Son of God!"

                                          . . . Sunday's coming!

It's Sunday   The angel in dazzling light rolled away the stone proclaiming to the world,
"He is not here! He is risen!"

It's Sunday! It's Sunday!! It's Sunday!!! It's Sunday today!!!

ABOUT COOKING THAT TURKEY

Worried about cooking that Thanksgiving turkey? It's no big deal if you follow a few straightforward rules, say the kindergarten students at Rue Elementary School in Council Bluffs, Iowa.

"Cut his head off. Cook him," David Rooney said. "Get his feathers off. I wouldn't like to eat that! Cut his feet off."

Zachary Kirk said it doesn't take long to cook the bird, but be sure to pay attention to the eyeballs. Cook it for 10 minutes. Stir up the turkey. Take it out of the oven, cut it in half and poke the eyeballs out. Set the plates, forks and knives on the table. Then eat it."

The children disagreed on how long to cook the turkey. Breanne Butterfield said it's a snap. "Wash it off. Put flour on it. Put it in the oven for one second," she said.

Samantha Garrison was insistent it takes a little longer. "Put it in the oven. check on it. Take the skin off. Put it back in the pan. Check it and stir on it. After 50 hours, check it again."

Basting is important, said Destyni Summer. "Put some salt on it, then some pepper on it. Put some apple juice on it and then some pears. Add sugar. Put some pumpkin seeds on the turkey. Put it in the oven."

No need to call 1-800-Help-Me-Cook-This-Bird. It's easy, said Mitchell Herrick. "Put milk in it. Put a little meat in the turkey. Cook it for 15 hours or so," he said.

See? Simple.

THE *WORK* OF *CHRISTMAS*

When the song of the angels is stilled,

When the star in the sky is gone,

When the kings and princes are home,

When the shepherds are back with their flock,
    the work of Christmas begins:

        To find the lost,

         To heal the broken,

         To feed the hungry,

         To release the prisoner,

         To rebuild the nations,

         To bring peace among brothers,

         To make music in the heart.

IF WE HAD NEEDED...

If we had needed knowledge,
> He would have sent us an educator.

If we had needed health,
> He would have sent us a doctor.

If we had needed wisdom,
> He would have sent us a philosopher.

If we had needed harmony,
> He would have sent us a musician.

If we had needed wealth,
> He would have sent us an economist.

If we had needed success,
> He would have sent us an efficiency expert.

But we needed a Saviour.
> He sent us Jesus.

> A thousand times in history, a baby has become a King,
> but only once in history did a King become a baby.

MURPHY'S LAW...
Christmas Syle

The time it takes to find a parking place is inversely proportional to the amount of time you have to spend.

The more expensive a breakable gift is, the better the chances of dropping it.

The other line always moves faster.

Unassembled toys will have twice as many screws as you expect, and some will always be left over.

Interchangeable parts aren't.

All children have built-in detection devices when it comes to finding the Christmas gifts you've so cleverly hidden.

Amnesia strikes all family members when the Scotch tape and scissors can't be found.

When a broken toy is demonstrated for the Store Manager, it works perfectly.

SECTION TWELVE

Seniors

YOU KNOW YOU'RE GETTING **OLD** WHEN ...

... your knees buckle, and your belt won't.

... you sit down in a rocking chair and can't get it started.

... your back goes out more often than you do.

... you know all the answers but nobody asks you any questions.

... your mind makes agreements your body can't meet.

... you finally get it all together . . .
        and then you can't remember where you put it.

... you can't even get around to procrastinating.

... everything hurts . . . and what doesn't hurt, doesn't work.

... you stop to think and sometimes forget to start again.

... resisting temptation is not as hard as recognizing it.

... you go into a record store and expect to see records.

... you're 17 around the neck, 40 around the waist and 126 around the
        golf course.

... anything under a quarter isn't worth bending over to pick up.

REMEMBER WHEN . . .

..... the only hazard presented by insecticides was running into the flypaper?

...... A marriage was likely to outlast all three wedding present toasters?

...... A drug problem was trying to get a prescription filled on Sunday?

. ... The postman not only rang twice, he delivered twice?

..... Bicycles and chickens came fully assembled?

..... The quality of music wasn't measured in decibels?

..... A whole family could go to the movies for what it now costs for the bag of popcorn?

THE 7 AGES OF MAN

At 20 he wants to wake up romantic.

At 30 he wants to wake up married.

At 40 he wants to wake up successful.

At 50 he wants to wake up rich.

At 60 he wants to wake up contented.

At 70 he wants to wake up healthy.

At 80 he wants to wake up.

MEN...
AND ALUMINUM CANS

At 10... we think we should save aluminum cans.

At 20... we think we should save the world.

At 30... we think we should save the company.

At 40... we think we should save our children.

At 50... we think we should save our marriage.

At 60... we think we should save our job.

At 70... we think we should save aluminum cans.

SPEED OF TIME BY AGE

00-09: Extremely slow. Even a trip to the store with Mom seems like going to Albania... by covered wagon. Most common phrase: "Is it Christmas yet?"

10-19: Still slow. Scientific evidence mounts that school clocks actually move backward before the bell rings.

20-29: Alternately fast and slow. Weekends seem shorter and shorter, yet paychecks seem further and further apart.

30-39: Time achieves warp speed, except when you are put on hold on the telephone and forced to endure anything longer than 1.8 seconds of Muzak. Most common phrase: "Is it Christmas already?"

40-49: Still fast. Seems like it was just yesterday when Jerry Brown said he might run for president. Wait a minute! It was yesterday. Also, Dick Clark still looks the same. Could time be slowing down?

60-69: What happened to 50-59?

70 plus: Unbelievably fast. Wars used to last years. Now they seem to be over in a couple of weeks.

DON'T BLAME THEM

Senior Citizens are constantly being criticized belittled and sniped at for every conceivable deficiency of the modern world... real and imaginary.

Upon reflection, let it be pointed out that it wasn't the seniors citizens who took the melody out of music,

or the beauty out of art,

or the pride out of appearance,

or the romance out of love,

the commitment out of marriage,

the responsibility out of parenthood,

togetherness out of family,

learning out of education,

loyalty out of Americanism,

service out of patriotism,

the hearth out of the home,

civility out of behavior,

refinement out of language,

dedication out of employment,

prudence out of spending,

or ambition out of achievement.

And they certainly are not the ones who eliminated patience and tolerance from relationships.

$\mathcal{P}$ROFILE OF A $\mathcal{S}$ENIOR

We were here before the Pill and the population explosion.

... before TV
    penicillin
    polio shots
    antibiotics
    open-heart surgery
    and hair transplants.

... before frozen food
        nylon
        Dacron
        Xerox
        Kinsey
        radar
        fluorescent lights
        credit cards
        ball point pens
        and Frisbees.

For us time sharing meant togetherness, not computers or condos.

Co-eds never wore slacks.

We were before panty hose
        drip-dry clothes
        ice makers
        dishwashers
        clothes dryers
        freezers
        and electric blankets.

        Before Hawaii and Alaska became states
        and before men wore long hair
        and earrings
        or before women wore tuxedos.

We were before Leonard Bernstein
        Ann Landers
        plastic
        the 40-hour week
        and minimum wages.

        We got married first
        and then lived together
        and then had babies.

Closets were for hanging clothes in, not for coming out of.

We were before Grandma Moses
        The Lone Ranger
        Frank Sinatra
        Batman
    and Mickey Mouse.

                    All the girls wore Peter Pan collars
                and thought cleavage was what butchers did.

We were before vitamins
            disposable diapers
            Jeeps
            pizza
            face-lifts
            Cheerios
                instant coffee
                decaffinated anything
                and McDonalds's .

    We thought fast food was what you ate during Lent.

We were before Chiquita bananas
                FM radios
                tape recorders
                electric typewriters
                boom boxes
                word processors
                electronic music
                disco dancing
                computer dating
                and commuter marriages.

For us time-sharing meant togetherness . . . not computers
                        or condominiums.
                A chip meant a piece of wood,
                    hardware meant hardware
                and software wasn't even a word.

    In our day, grass was for mowing
            Coke was for drinking
            and pot was something you cooked in.

If we had been asked to explain CIA
                UFO
                VCR
                MBA
                BMW
        and NFL, we'd have said, "ALPHABET SOUP."

THEY SAID WHAT... WHEN?

It is only when you have lost your teeth that you can afford to eat steak!

Pierre Renoir, French painter

All would live long, but none would be old. **Benjamin Franklin**
POOR RICHARD'S ALMANACK

Oh, what I wouldn't give to be 70 again!

Justice Oliver Wendell Homles, 92,
upon seeing an attractive woman

To see a young couple loving each other is a wonder; but to see an old couple loving each other is the best sight of all. **William Makepeace Thackeray**

Growing old is no more than a bad habit which a busy man has no time to form.

Old age is not for sissies. **Katharine Hepburn**

I believe that one has to be seventy before one is full of courage. The young are always half-hearted. **D. H. Lawrence**

To be 70 years young is sometimes far more cheerful than to be forty years old.

Oliver Wendell Holmes
in a letter to Julia Ward Howe
on her 70th birthday, 1889

I promise to keep on living as though I expected to live forever. Nobody grows old by merely living a number of years. People grow old by deserting their ideals. Years may wrinkle the skin, but to give up interest wrinkles the soul.

General Douglas MacArthur
on his 75th birthday
January 26, 1955

"Old age isn't so bad when you consider the alternative.

Maurice Chevalier
at age 72

Most people say that as you get old, you have to give things up. I say you get old because you give things up. **U.S. Senator Theodore Francis Green**
on his 87th birthday

I am interested in physical medicine because my father was. I am interested in arthritis because I have it. **Bernard M. Baruch**
89 in 1959

I'm sixty-five, and I guess that puts me in with the geriatrics. But if there were fifteen months in a year, I would only be forty-eight. **James Thurber**

The years between fifty and seventy are the hardest. You are always being asked to do things and yet you are not decrepit enough to turn them down.

T. S. Eliot

Section
Thirteen

....

SERVICE

Selective Service... MAY I HELP YOU?

Which stranded motorist gets help the soonest... a pregnant woman, a little old lady, a messy hippie, a smartly dressed career woman or a sexy siren?

A Space Coast newspaper decided to find out, and ran a test on Florida's U.S. Route 1 with a 22-year-old actress, Sally Mullins, playing the driver in distress in all five roles.

CAREER WOMAN: Dressed in a double-breasted suit she stood by her "hood-up, broken-down" Pontiac Grand Am, holding a "stop" sign and waited for help. A minute and a half and 62 vehicles later, Bill Leonardi pulled over to offer assistance.

PREGNANT WOMAN: Disguised with about 8 months of padding, she had to wait 2 1/2 minutes while more than 100 cars whizzed past before paramedics Bob Smith and Dorothy Jenning (who had been driving in the opposite direction) made a U-turn in their ambulance to lend Sally a helping hand.

LITTLE OLD LADY: She had to wait nearly 5 minutes and watch 200 vehicles drive by before two people pulled over to help her... 22-year-old college co-ed Glenna Newell and land surveyor Greg Smith, 29.

HIPPIE GIRL: Costumed in faded jeans, a loud floral blouse and wild blonde wig, nobody stopped at all! She stood by her car for more than 15 minutes while over 350 cars, trucks, vans, buses and motorcycles zoomed by. No one even slowed down.

MINI-SKIRTED NYMPH IN NEED: Sally no sooner put up the hood of her car when Ed Kent of West Palm Beach barreled to a stop right behind her. That "damsel in distress" outfit stopped a car in 9 seconds... the fastest of any of them!

STICK TO IT!

I represent my country.

I'm always ready for service.

I go wherever I'm sent.

I do what I'm asked to do.

I stick to my task until it's done.

I don't strike back when I'm struck.

I don't give up when I'm licked.

I'm necessary to the happiness of the world.

I keep up to date.

I find no job too small.

I work well on a team for big jobs.

I'm crowned with a mark of service.

I am a Postage Stamp!!

Who Lost The Game?

Behold a ball team went forth to play a game of baseball. Just as the umpire was saying "BATTER UP" the catcher for the home team arrived and took his place.

The center fielder didn't arrive until the end of the first inning and the second baseman didn't get there until the second inning had already started.

The first baseman didn't show up at all, but later sent his regrets and said that he had to go to a chicken dinner at his Aunt Amy's.

And the third baseman failed to come to the game because he had been up late the night before and needed to catch up on sleep.

The left fielder felt the need to visit another ball game across town.

The shortstop was present . . . but left his glove at home.

Two of the substitute fielders were away on a week-end trip and couldn't make it. But they were there in spirit.

Verily, when the pitcher went to the mound, he looked around for his teammates, and lo, his heart was heavy, for their places were empty. But the game was announced and the visitors were there in the stands, and there was nothing to do but to pitch the game and hope for the best.

So the pitcher tightened his belt and stepped into the box and did his best to put the ball over the plate. But he was not at his best, because he had to serve as pitcher, first baseman and third basemen all at the same time.

There were loud "boos" from the stands when the home team was badly beaten. It was a disgrace to the noble game of baseball. When the absent members of the defeated team heard that their team lost, a decision was made to get a new pitcher.

But who really lost the game?

There is no substitute for faithfulness.

HAPPY ARE THE...

Happy are the pushy...
>> for they get on in the world.

✦ ✦ ✦

Happy are the hard-boiled...
>> for they never let life hurt them.

✦ ✦ ✦

Happy are those who complain...
>> for they get their own way.

✦ ✦ ✦

Happy are the blase'...
>> for they never worry over their sins.

✦ ✦ ✦

Happy are the slave drivers...
>> for they get results.

✦ ✦ ✦

Happy are the knowledgeable...
>> for they know their way around.

✦ ✦ ✦

Happy are the trouble makers...
>> for people take notice of them.

NOT!!!

GUERILLA GOODNESS

It's a crisp winter day in San Francisco. A woman in a red Honda, Christmas presents piled in the back, drives up to the Bay Bridge tollbooth. "I'm paying for myself... and for the six cars behind me," she announces with a smile, handing over seven commuter tickets.

One after another, the next six drivers arrive at the tollbooth, dollars in hand, only to be told, "Some lady in a red car up ahead of you already paid your fare. Have a nice day."

The woman in the red Honda, it turned out, had read something on an index card taped to a friend's refrigerator: "Practice random kindness and senseless acts of beauty." The phrase seemed to leap out at her, and she copied it down.

Now the phrase is spreading, on bumper stickers, on walls, at the bottom of letters and business cards. And as it spreads, so does a vision of guerilla goodness.

In Portland, Oregon, a man plunks a coin into a stranger's parking meter just in time.

In Paterson, New Jersey, a dozen people with pails and mops and tulip bulbs descend on a run-down house and clean it from top to bottom while the frail elderly owners look on, dazed and smiling.

In Grand Rapids, a teenage boy is shoveling off his driveway when the impulse strikes. He thinks nobody's looking... so he shovels the neighbor's driveway, too.

Happiness is like jam... you can't spread even a little without getting some on yourself. Likewise you can't commit a random kindness without feeling as if your own troubles have been lightened if only because the world has become a slightly better place.

Like all revolutions, guerilla goodness begins slowly, with a single act. Let it be yours.

Section Fourteen

SUCCESS

HOW TO SUCCEED WITHOUT COLLEGE

You can reach the top in business and life regardless of your education . . . and here are the best ways to do it.

1. <u>**WORK "CAN'T SEE" HOURS**</u>. Start work when it's so dark you can't see and finish when you can't see because it's dark again.

   Bill Rosenburg,
   Dunkin' Donuts founder

2. <u>**LOVE WHAT YOU DO . . . AND DO IT!**</u> Don't procrastinate. And don't think. Do it. Thinking is the enemy of creativity. You can't think about things. You simply must DO them.

   Ray Bradbury
   Science Fiction author

3. <u>**GIVE THE CUSTOMER VALUE FOR THE MONEY**</u>. Putting a good product at a reasonable price in front of a customer likely means he'll come back. And if he does, your business is a success.

   Harold Butler
   Founder of Denny's

4. <u>**START SMALL**</u>. Set short-term goals. Great dreams are often so far away from your reach that you can become discouraged. But each small goal you achieve gives you confidence to try the next.

   John H. Johnson
   Publisher of Ebony

5. <u>**DON'T LET OTHER PEOPLE'S NEGATIVE ATTITUDES WORK AGAINST YOU**</u>. Tune those people out. Listen to your heart, believe in your abilities, work harder than ever . . . and you will accomplish your dreams.

   Regine Choukroun
   Founder of Regine's Clubs

6. **BELIEVE THAT NOTHING IS IMPOSSIBLE.** It doesn't matter how many times you fail in trying to get something to work. All you need is one success.

Jack Goeken
Founder of MCI Telephone Network

7. **TRY TO LEARN FROM OTHER PEOPLE.** Then once you get a good grasp of what is going on, say what's on your mind and do what you think is right. Your goal should always be to be the very best at what you do.

Jay Darling
President of Burger King

8. **FIND A NEED AND FILL IT.** But never resort to gimmicks! If you fill a real need, you'll have a loyal following.

Adrien Arpel
Cosmetics Queen

9. **KEEP YOUR WORD.** If you say you'll do something, do it. What is needed . . . and wanted . . . in the world are people who will do what they say they'll do. And think really big. If you have the courage to stand up and say, "This is what I want to do," and do it, you can be successful.

William Millard
Founder of ComputerLand

10. **LEARN FROM YOUR MISTAKES.** Too many people, when they make a mistake, just keep stubbornly plowing ahead and end up repeating the same mistakes. I believe in the motto, "Try and try again." But the way I read it, it says, "Try, then stop and think. Then try again."

William Dean Singleton
Co-owner of MediaNews Group Inc.

11 **SET YOUR PRIORITIES.** Seek ye first the kingdom of God and His righteousness, and all these [good] things shall be added unto you.

Jesus Christ
Owner of the Universe

The World's Richest Man... POOR GUY!

The wealthiest man on the face of the earth is the Sultan of Brunei, whose has a personal fortune of $37 billion. Incredibly, the ruler of this tiny Muslim nation admits he's miserable... even though he lives in an $800,000,000 palace complete with 1,876 rooms...

... including a throne room seating 2,000 people,

... with air-conditioned stables,

... a heliport,

... a polo field,

... 300 acres of landscaped gardens,

... and a 700 car garage.

He owns 250 fancy cars, but there is nowhere for him to drive because nearly every street dead-ends into the surrounding jungle... and on the few roads that do go somewhere, the traffic is so slow he can never go fast enough to get out of third gear.

He owns a giant yacht... one of the largest in the world... but he gets seasick every time he steps aboard.

He has a personal jet, a Boeing 727, and he flies in it every day... but all he does is make a giant circle and return home. His kingdom is so small it has only one airport big enough for the plane to land.

And he has twenty-two wives (allowed by Muslim law) who are so jealous of each other that they make his life a living hell with constant, jealous bickering. To placate his spouses, he built quarters for each wife. So now he sleeps alone...and drives his Rolls-Royce six miles to visit them.

DOLLAR DEFINITION

Workers earn it

$

Spendthrifts burn it

$

Bankers lend it

$

Women spend it

$

Forgers fake it

$

Taxes take it

$

Dying leave it

$

Heirs receive it

$

Thrifty save it

$

Misers crave it

$

Robbers seize it

$

Rich increase it

$

Gamblers lose it

$

I could use it

SAYINGS FROM
POOR RICHARD'S ALMANACK

If you would not be forgotten
As soon as you are dead and rotten,
Either write things worth the reading,
Or do things worth the writing.

❦❦❦

Doing an injury puts you below your enemy.
Revenging one makes you but even with him.
Forgiving it sets you above him.

❦❦❦

All would live long, but none would be old.

❦❦❦

Having been poor is no shame, but being ashamed of it is.

❦❦❦

Write injuries in dust, benefits in marble.

Section Fifteen

Words

SIGNED IN TORTURED ENGLISH

(TELL IT LIKE IT ISN'T)

A Prague shop boasts that the store's pigskin wallets are "made of pure pork."

Guests in a Czechoslovakian hotel room are greeted with this notice about the TV: "If the set brakes, inform manager, do not interfere with yourself."

A Romanian hotel warns guests that the elevator "is being fixed for the next day. During that time we regret that you will be unbearable."

How could any tourist in Prague resist this posted come-on: "Take one of our horse-driven city tours . . . we guarantee no miscarriages."

A Bulgarian beach sign warns, "Women wearing topless suits will be put into the hands of authorities."

One East Berlin store tells shoppers: "Give your husband a belt" and another invites them to "Visit our bargain basement one flight up."

A laundry in romantic Italy suggests: "Ladies, leave your clothes here and spend the afternoon having a good time."

A Greek tailor shop declares: "Because is big rush we will execute customers in strict rotation."

The menu of a Swiss restaurant brags that: "Our wines leave you nothing to hope for."

An elevator in Paris advises: "Please leave your values at the front desk."

A quiet Oslo cocktail lounge states: "Ladies are requested not to have children in the bar."

An Acapulco hotel ominously guarantees: "The manager has personally passed the water served here."

Spotted on the bottom of a menu in Tokyo: "These items may or may not be available at all times and sometimes not at all and other times all the time."

Superfluous Verbosity

Members of an avian species of identical plumage congregate.

BIRDS OF A FEATHER FLOCK TOGETHER.

Surveillance should precede salation.

LOOK BEFORE YOUR LEAP.

It is fruitless to become lachrymose over precipitately departed lacteal fluid.

NO USE CRYING OVER SPILLED MILK.

Freedom from incrustations of grime is contiguous to rectitude.

CLEANLINESS IS NEXT TO GODLINESS.

The temperature of the aqueous content of an unremittingly ogled saucepan does not reach 212 degrees Fahrenheit.

A WATCHED POT NEVER BOILS.

All articles that coruscate with resplendence are not truly auriferous.

ALL THAT GLITTERS IS NOT GOLD.

Eleemosynary deeds have their incipience intramurally.

CHARITY BEGINS AT HOME.

Neophyte's serendipity.

BEGINNER'S LUCK.

The person presenting the ultimate cachinnation possesses thereby the optimal cachinnation.

HE WHO LAUGHS LAST, LAUGHS BEST.

Abstention from undertakings precludes a potent escalation of a profitable nature.

NOTHING VENTURED, NOTHING GAINED.

Pulchritude possesses solely cutaneous profundity.

BEAUTY IS ONLY SKIN DEEP.

The stylus is more potent than the claymore.

THE PEN IS MIGHTIER THAN THE SWORD.

Scintillate, scintillate asteroid minific.

TWINKLE, TWINKLE, LITTLE STAR.

Achieve analysis of your feathered appendages.

TRY YOUR WINGS.

Diamonds in the ROUGH

Baseball players don't just throw curves and make errors on the ball field...
many do it when they speak... and the results are hilarious.

Yogi Berra explaining why attendance was down in Kansas City...
**IF PEOPLE DON'T WANT TO COME OUT TO THE PARK,
NOBODY'S GOING TO STOP THEM."**

Yogi Berra's son Dale's reply when asked to compare himself to his famous father...
OUR SIMILARITIES ARE DIFFERENT.

Dave Henderson's answer to a reporter when questioned about going to bat 40 times
before getting on base...
I WASN'T IN A SLUMP... I JUST WASN'T GETTING ANY HITS.

Manager Casey Stengle's remark during an Old-Timers' Game in which he teamed
up with stars he used to play against...
**IT'S WONDERFUL TO MEET SO MANY FRIENDS I DIDN'T USED
TO LIKE.**

Slugger Willie Stargell 's observation about what it was like to bat against fast-baller
Sandy Koufax...
**TRYING TO HIT HIM IS LIKE TRYING TO DRINK YOUR
COFFEE WITH A FORK.**

Elrod Hendricks' reply when asked about manager Earl Weaver's mood...
**YOU KNOW EARL. HE'S NOT HAPPY UNLESS HE'S NOT
HAPPY.**

Pedro Guerrero during an interview in which he criticized sports writers...
**SOMETIMES THEY WRITE WHAT I SAY AND NOT WHAT I
MEAN.**

Umpire Dick Stello was once told he couldn't have seen whether a ball hit 250 feet
away was fair or foul...
**ON A CLEAR DAY I CAN SEE THE SUN, AND THAT SUCKER IS
93 MILLION MILES AWAY.**

THE WORD IS...

The greatest word is .... **God**

The longest word is .... **Eternity**

The swiftest word is............................... **Time**

The nearest word is .... **Now**

The bitterest word is .... **Alone**

The darkest word is .... **Sin**

The cruelest word is .... **Revenge**

The meanest word is....................... **Hypocrisy**

The saddest word is .... **Lost**

The dearest word is........................... **Mother**

The sweetest word is.............................. **Jesus**

The deepest word is .... **Soul**

The coldest word is....................................**No**

The most desirable word is....................... **Life**

The most tragic word is .... **Death**

The most beautiful word is .... **Love**

The most compelling word is .... **Faith**

The most comforting word is .... **Hope**

Upon My Word

We all seem to be hung up on UP

We put up with use up
come up
butter up
line up
punch up
and belly up

Houses are opened up
lighted up
warmed up
cleaned up
and closed up

Motors are fired up
gassed up
and charged up

Boats are speeded up
slowed up
tied up
and laid up

If we are mixed up
we must hurry up
and shape up
or we'll be fouled up

And heaven help us
we drink up
with 7-UP

If you think up other examples
don't call me up

I'm up the wall with UP

I give up!

LETTER PERFECT

The letter "E" is always out of cash
forever in debt
never out of danger
and always in trouble

It is never in war
but always in peace

It is the beginning and end of existence
and the center of honesty

Even though it starts off in error
it does end by making life complete

And most important of all...
without it...
there would be no love.

NEWSPAPER HEADLINE BLOOPERS

MAN SURVIVED 17 DAYS ADRIFT ON FLYING FISH

Los Angeles Times

SISTERS REUNITED AFTER 18 YEARS IN CHECKOUT LINE AT SUPERMARKET

The Arkansas Democrat

CROWDS RUSHING TO SEE POPE TRAMPLE 6 TO DEATH

Journal Star (Peoria, IL)

CHEF THROWS HIS HEART INTO HELPING FEED THE NEEDY

Louisville Courier-Journal

FRIED CHICKEN COOKED IN MICROWAVE WINS TRIP

The Oregonian (Portland)

BLIND WOMAN GETS NEW KIDNEY FROM LADY SHE HASN'T SEEN IN YEARS

Alabama Journal

RED TAPE HOLDS UP NEW BRIDGE

Milford Citizen (CT)

ANTI-NUDITY LAW TO GET CLOSER LOOK

Capital-Journal/Topeka, Kansas

English Anguish
ADS THAT ADD

෨෨෨

DINNER SPECIAL
Turkey $2.35
Chicken or Beef $2.25
Children $2.00

෨෨෨

OUR BIKINIS ARE EXCITING.
They Are Simply the Tops

෨෨෨

ILLITERATE?
Write today for free help.

෨෨෨

WANTED
Unmarried girls to pick fresh fruit
and produce at night

෨෨෨

SEMI-ANNUAL AFTER-CHRISTMAS SALE

SAYS WHO?

Philosophers are people who talk about something they don't understand and make you think it's your fault.

Greece said,	"Be wise.	Know yourself!"
Rome said,	"Be strong.	Discipline yourself!"
Religion says,	"Be good.	Conform yourself!"
Epicureanism says,	"Be sensuous.	Enjoy yourself!"
Education says,	"Be resourceful.	Expand yourself!"
Psychology says,	"Be confident.	Assert yourself!"
Materialism says,	"Be satisfied.	Please yourself!"
Pride says,	"Be superior.	Promote yourself!"
Asceticism says,	"Be lowly.	Supress yourself!"
Humanism says,	"Be capable.	Believe yourself!"
Legalism says,	"Be pious.	Limit yourself!"
Philanthropy says,	"Be generous.	Release yourself!"
Jesus says,	"Be serving.	Give yourself!"

Science makes God unnecessary.
Philosophy makes God impossible.
Psychology makes God an illusion.
Communism makes God an enemy.
Capitalism makes God a convenience.
Novelists use Him as a vocabulary expander.

WHACKY EATERIES

FU'S RUSH INN   (Hewlett, NY)

MUSTARD'S LAST STAND   (Evanston, IL)

INN COGNITO   (Genoa, NV)

HUMPHREY YOGART   (Hammond, IN)

WOK RIGHT IN   (Indianapolis, IN)

HARD WOK CAFE   (Palm Springs, CA)

GARDEN OF EAT'N   (Santa Ana, CA)

SQUID ROE   (New York City)

DONUT BEAT ALL   (Wichita, KN)

WIFE SAVER   (Augusta, GA)

LETTUCE SOUPRISE YOU   (Atlanta, GA)

M.T. BELLI'S   (Clovis, NM)

DELI BELOVED   (Stevensville, MI)

WOK AND ROLL   (New York, NY)

BLAZING SALADS   (Dublin, Ireland)

SECTION SIXTEEN

The Work Place

New Sick Leave Policy

SICKNESS:

No excuse. We will no longer accept your doctor's statement as proof. We believe that if you are able to go to the doctor, you are able to come to work.

LEAVE OF ABSENCE (for an operation):

We are no longer allowing this practice. We wish to discourage any thought that you may have about needing an operation. We believe that as long as you are employed here, you will need all of whatever you have and should not consider having anything removed. We hired you as you are and to have anything removed would certainly make you less than we bargained for.

LEAVE OF ABSENCE (other personal needs):

Too much time is being spent in the Rest Room. In the future, we will follow the practice of going to the Rest Room in alphabetical order. For instance, those whose names begin with "A" will go from 8:00 to 8:05 A.M., "B" will go from 8:05 to 8:10 A.M., and so on. If you are unable to go at your time, it will be necessary to wait until the time of day when your turn comes again.

DEATH (other than your own):

This is no excuse. There is nothing you can do for them, and we are sure that someone else in a lesser position can attend to the arrangements. However, if the funeral can be held in the late afternoon, we will reluctantly (but generously) let you off one hour early, provided your share of work is ahead enough to keep the job going in your absence.

DEATH (your own):

This will be accepted as an excuse, but since we feel it is your duty to teach someone else your job, we will keep our policy of "two-weeks notice" in force.

Table of Handy Office Excuses

1. That's the way we've always done it.

2. I didn't know you were in a hurry for it.

3. That's not my department.

4. No one told me to go ahead.

5. I'm waiting for an O.K.

6. How did I know this was different?

7. That's his job, not mine.

8. Wait till the boss comes back and ask him.

9. We don't make many mistakes.

10. I didn't think it was very important.

11. I'm so busy, I just can't get around to it.

12. I thought I told you.

13. I wasn't hired to do that.

THE STRAIN OF THE DRAIN

Oh, the things that you find when you clean out a drain. Roto-Rooter Corp. surveyed 204 of its service technicians and asked what was the most uncommon item they had found in a clogged sewer or drainpipe.

A brick
a baseball
a beaver
a beeper

A padlock
a doorknob
a hummingbird feeder

An apple
a meatloaf
a steak
an orange

A muskrat
a cat
some missing bulls' horns

A bed sheet
some blue jeans
a live frog
and a fish.

And so far this barely scratches the list.

NO WONDER NOTHING GETS DONE AROUND HERE

Here are some absolutely irrefutable statistics that show exactly why you are tired. There aren't nearly as many people actually working as you may have thought, at least not according to this survey.

The population of this country is a little over 250,000,000.

84,000,000 are over 64 years of age and retired. That leaves 166,000,000 of us to do all the work.

People under 20 years of age total 95,000,000... so that leaves 71,000,000 to do the work.

There are 27,000,000 who are employed by the government, which leaves 44,000,000 to do the work.

14,000,000 are in the Armed Forces, which leaves 30,000,000 to do the work.

Deduct 20,000,000... the number in state and city offices. That leaves 10,000,000 to do the work.

There are 6,000,000 in hospitals, mental institutions and various asylums so that leaves 4,000,000 to do the work.

Now it may interest you to know that there are 3,999,998 people in jails and prisons... so that leaves just 2 people to carry the load.

That's you and me... and I'm about ready to take a vacation.

The Ultimate Staff Exam

1. LEADERSHIP QUOTIENT:
a. ( ) Leaps tall obstacles with a single bound
b. ( ) Must take a running start to leap over tall obstacles
c. ( ) Can leap over small obstacles
d. ( ) Crashes into obstacles when jumping over them
e. ( ) Cannot recognize obstacles at all

2. STRENGTH OF CHARACTER:
a. ( ) Is stronger than a herd of bulls
b. ( ) Is stronger than several bulls
c. ( ) Is stronger than one bull
d. ( ) Shoots the bull
e. ( ) Smells like a bull

3. PREACHING:
a. ( ) Enthralls huge throngs
b. ( ) Enthralls his congregation
c. ( ) Interests his congregation
d. ( ) Only his wife listens
e. ( ) Not even his wife listens

4. SPIRITUAL MATURITY:
a. ( ) Walks on water consistently
b. ( ) Walks on water in emergencies
c. ( ) Swims in water
d. ( ) Washes in water
e. ( ) Drinks water

5. COMMUNICATION:
a. ( ) Talks with God
b. ( ) Talks with angels
c. ( ) Talks to himself
d. ( ) Argues with himself
e. ( ) Loses arguments with himself

SO YOU WANT THE DAY OFF...
...LET'S LOOK WHAT YOU ARE ASKING FOR

1. There are 365 days in a year available for work.

2. There are 52 weeks in the year and you already have two days off for each weekend, leaving 261 days available for work.

3. Since you spend 16 hours each day away from work, you have used up 170 days, leaving only 91 days available.

4. You spend 30 minutes each day on coffee breaks, and that accounts for 23 days each year, leaving only 68 days available.

5. With a one hour lunch period each day, you have used up another 46 days, leaving only 22 days available for work.

6. You normally spend 2 days a year on sick leave. This now leaves you with only 20 days available for work.

7. We are off for 5 holidays every year, so your available working time has shrunk to 15 days.

8 We generously give you 14 days off for vacation each year which leaves only 1 day available for you to work for us.

9. If you think you're getting that day off too, you're absolutely crazy!

Topical
Index

SENIORS

SERVICE

SPORTS

SUCCESS

THANKSGIVING

WOMEN

WORDS

THE WORK PLACE